THE OXFORD BOOK OF AUSTRALIAN LIGHT VERSE

THE OXFORD BOOK OF *Australian* LIGHT VERSE

SELECTED BY
R.F. BRISSENDEN & PHILIP GRUNDY

OXFORD

OXFORD UNIVERSITY PRESS AUSTRALIA

Oxford New York Toronto Delhi Bombay Calcutta Madras
Karachi Petaling Jaya Singapore Hong Kong Tokyo Nairobi
Dar es Salaam Cape Town Melbourne Auckland
and associated companies in
Berlin Ibadan

First published 1991

National Library of Australia
Cataloguing-in-Publication data:

The Oxford book of Australian light verse.
Includes index.
ISBN 0 19 554512 5.

1. Humorous poetry, Australian. I. Brissenden, R. F. (Robert Francis), 1928–1991. II. Grundy, Philip.

A821.0708

Cover design by Jennifer Johnston
Typeset by Solo Typesetting, South Australia
Printed by Brown Prior Anderson, Victoria
Published by Oxford University Press, 253 Normanby Road, South Melbourne, Australia

Contents

Foreword

The selection of verse for this anthology was originally a task undertaken with enthusiasm by my late friend and colleague Dr R. F. (Bob) Brissenden. Many of the poems included were offered in response to a letter which he sent to his exceptionally wide range of friends and acquaintances among Australian poets.

Sadly, however, the debilitating illness which Bob suffered and endured so bravely and patiently, made it impossible for him to deal physically with the task of compiling the anthology. He asked me if I would join him in the work and I gladly undertook to do so. Apart from the poems that were submitted by their authors, including some previously unpublished works, there are many from collected works and anthologies. I am grateful to Professor Chris Wallace-Crabbe for his help in steering me towards some of these.

It had also been Bob's intention to write an essay on light verse by way of an introduction to this volume. On the day before he died, we discussed the question of the introduction and were to meet the following week to consider the draft which he had in mind. My own observations are by no means an attempt to substitute for what so distinguished a scholar and critic as Bob Brissenden might have written. At best I can describe the basis we used for selection and mention some of the points that he and I were agreed upon.

The first point that Bob would have made—as he said to me several times—was that light verse does not have to be funny, either in intention or in execution. Its purpose may be very serious: to make the reader think, to challenge received opinions, or to assert an unpopular point of view. What is essential, however, is that the form of verse be light, for in poetry as in cooking, a light touch may prove to offer the greatest satisfaction.

It is not the intention here to deliver a weighty essay on the nature of light verse, or to attempt to distinguish it from satire, comic verse, or parody. Lightness in verse is something that the reader recognises but is hard pressed to define. The same may be said of other arts. It seems true nonetheless that strict rhythm and rhyme are not essential to the genre, even though most successful light verse may use these traditional devices to produce a sense of inevitability—of the right thing said in the right way. On the other hand, light verse is almost always marked by a clever manipulation of words: however serious its intent may be, its hallmark must be that of wit.

That opinion leads to another concerning the sources of light verse. If light verse is not to become heavy verse, and I would include satire in that category, it needs to exhibit a certain detachment, a kind of benign observation which does not treat life flippantly but at the same time refuses to take the human race and its follies too seriously. This of course can easily lead to arrogance and frequently what purports to be light verse may fail because the writer displays too openly a sense of superiority to, if not contempt for, poor, struggling humanity.

Yet not every generation can breed the kind of poet capable of that benign and affectionate detachment. Times of war, depression, and political and social upheaval are all too serious for light-hearted treatment. These are times of bitter and savage satire rather than of light verse. In the short period during which the English language has prevailed in Australia, there have not been too many times when the nation's poets have felt sufficiently detached about public affairs to treat them lightly; thus most of the poems in this anthology are relatively recent.

Naturally, there have always been subjects in any age which lent themselves to light verse, but these have tended in Australia to restrict the genre to certain interest-groups. One great Australian tradition of verse is that of the 'bush ballads' and the like: folk poetry which alleviated the desperately hard conditions of bush-dwellers by casting a humorous eye on their lot and eased the soul of the urban population (always in the great majority) by reinforcing a comforting rural myth. This tradition can truly be called light verse in great part, but we have not drawn much upon it here, partly because it sits uncomfortably with more sophisticated verse, but mainly because it has already been very extensively anthologised.

Those, on the other hand, who have practised the long-standing English language tradition of light verse have tended to be people who are, by profession or inclination, steeped in the British tradition from which it derives—that is to say, teachers and academics. A survey of published Australian poets outside the bush ballad stream would probably show a remarkable proportion of secondary and tertiary teachers of English.

There is, of course, nothing surprising, or wrong, about this; but it does lead to one unfortunate result for the writing of light verse. Because Australian poets tend to share a common profession, much of their light verse is concerned with academic preoccupations. Indeed, in searching for material for this anthology, I have been struck with the remarkable number of poems which parody or refer to other poets and their work. However witty and effective these poems may have been, I have generally rejected them, or at least required them to be of outstanding merit if they were to be included. Poems written as essentially private jokes among a small group of acquaintances or colleagues do not seem to suit an anthology designed for the general public.

Two other categories of exclusion seem also to require justification, if only because of the quantity in which they exist. The first is political verse. The rambunctious nature of Australian politics has produced a rich vein of verse, mocking, satirical and savagely sarcastic. Much of it was devastatingly effective; but when the events pilloried have faded from public memory, the sting goes out of it and the reader is left wondering what all the fuss was about. Who were these people the poet attacked, and why were they the victims of such calumny? There exist some excellent anthologies of such verse, but they necessarily contain such a copious quantity of footnotes and explanation before they can be fully savoured that it has not seemed advisable to include many examples here, even when the poems might otherwise have been regarded as good pieces of light verse. The other category is that of song texts. Much political verse was designed to be sung to tunes of the day, and Australians have long been adept at this form of composition. Bob Brissenden himself was no mean hand at this kind of thing (his 'Walking Through Canberra' with its chorus line: 'I'm a New South Wales copper, I can't tell a lie' is a classic of its kind), but again the same objections apply as to political verse—with the additional objection that most of these songs have to be sung to be appreciated. In cold print, the flavour vanishes.

It may be objected at this stage that the present collection excludes more than it includes; and in a way the charge is just. Bob Brissenden and I, however, were aware that other anthologies exist which contain voluminous quantities of bush ballads and of satirical, political and comic verse and song; and we did not set out to raid anthologies to create yet another one.

Our object has been to present a selection of light verse which certainly has a strong Australian flavour but which nevertheless lies in the same general tradition of the familiar work of British and North American poets. In selecting these poems we have been pleasantly surprised both by the amount of good light verse we have discovered and by the people who have written it successfully—some of them generally regarded as very serious poets indeed.

Ultimately, however, the poems have not so much been selected to fulfil certain preconceived criteria; rather the criteria have been drawn up to justify exclusions. The selection itself was based on vaguely perceived principles, but much more on the response to the simple question: Do I like this poem? As Kingsley Amis remarked at the end of a lengthy and scholarly disquisition in his introduction to *The New Oxford Book of Light Verse*, 'Perhaps my taste is at fault, but the whole of this volume is at the mercy of that taste . . .'

Philip Grundy
Canberra, 1991

In memory of Bob Brissenden
1928–1991

Anonymous

Sausage Wrap Serenade

(Tune: Drunken Sailor)

What shall we put in the daily paper?
What shall we put in the daily paper?
What shall we put in the daily paper?
Early in the morning?

Students in the road who riot,
Labor boys who won't keep quiet,
Newssheet boys who chance to spy it
Early in the morning.

Workers on the dole who guzzle,
Communists who need a muzzle,
Winners of a crossword puzzle
Early in the morning.

Suicide of a linen draper,
Duchess poisoned by noxious vapour,
Lady of eighty chased by raper
Early in the morning.

Awful international crisis,
Idiot reader wins three prizes,
See how the general public rises
Early in the morning.

Shove it all down in the daily paper;
Cabinet Minister cuts a caper,
Architect felled by his own skyscraper
Early in the morning.

Some of it's truth and some of it's lying,
What's the odds if the public's buying?
Editors never leave off trying
Early in the morning.

The Song of the RSL

(Tune: Advance Australia Fair)

Australia's sons let us rejoice
For we are young and white,
The yellow hordes may get us soon
But we are in the right.
The white man's burdens never cease,
We bear them night and day
Until the Asian hordes increase
And everybody's grey.

Chorus

Of mingled strains let others sing
But keep Australia white.

Though other races interbreed
We'll toil with heart and hand
To keep our island continent
A white and open land.
Our natives have their settlements,
Our neighbours are all Asian,
We'll sing and dance and wave our flags
Because we are Caucasian.

Though other states desegregate
Our gallant lads ensure
That through our British ancestry
Our heritage is pure.
The negroid races may prevail
But still Australians stand
United to this common end,
A white and pleasant land.

Marcus Clarke

The Wail of the Waiter

(A Tavern Catch)

All day long, at Scott's or Menzies', I await the gorging crowd,
Panting, penned within a pantry, with the blowflies humming loud.
There at seven in the morning do I count my daily cash,
While the home-returning reveller calls for 'soda and a dash'.
And the weary hansom-cabbies set the blinking squatters down,
Who, all night, in savage freedom, have been 'knocking round the town'.
Soon the breakfast gong resounding bids the festive meal begin,
And, with appetites like demons, come the gentle public in.
'Toast and butter!' 'Eggs and coffee!' 'Waiter, mutton chops for four!'
'Flatheads!' 'Ham!' 'Beef!' 'Where's the mustard?' 'Steak and onions!' 'Shut the door!'
Here sits Bandicoot, the broker, eating in a desperate hurry,
Scowling at his left-hand neighbour, Cornstalk from the Upper Murray,
Who with brandy-nose empurpled, and with blue lips cracked and dry,
In incipient delirium shoves the eggspoon in his eye.
'Bloater paste!' 'Some *tender* steak, sir?' 'Here, *confound* you, where's my chop?'
'Waiter!' 'Yessir!' '*Waiter!*' 'Yessir!!'—running till I'm fit to drop.
Then at lunch time—fearful crisis! In by shoals the gorgers pour,
Gobbling, crunching, swilling, munching—ten times hungrier than before.
'Glass of porter!' '*Ale* for me, John!' 'Where's my stick?' 'And where's my *hat*!'
'Oxtail soup!' '*I* asked for curry!' 'Cold boiled beef, and cut it fat!'
'Irish stew!' 'Some pickled cabbage!' 'What, no *beans*?' 'Bring *me* some pork!'
'Soup, sir?' 'Yes. You grinning idiot, can I eat it with a FORK?'
'Take care, waiter!' Beg your pardon. 'Curse you, have you two left legs?'
'I asked for *bread* an hour ago, sir!' 'Now then, have you *laid* those eggs?'
'Sherry!' 'No, I called for *beer*—of all the fools I ever saw!'

'Waiter!' 'Yessir!' 'WAITER!!' 'Here, sir!' 'Damme, sir, this steak
is RAW!'

Thus amid this hideous Babel do I live the livelong day,
While my memory is going, and my hair is turning grey.
All my soul is slowly melting, all my brain is softening fast,
And I know that I'll be taken to the Yarra Bend at last.
For at night from fitful slumbers I awaken with a start,
Murmuring of steak and onions, babbling of apple tart.
While to me the Poet's cloudland a gigantic kitchen seems,
And those mislaid table-napkins haunt me even in my dreams.
Is this right?—Ye sages tell me!—Does a man live but to eat?
Is there nothing worth enjoying but one's miserable meat?
Is the mightiest task of Genius but to swallow buttered beans,
And has Man but been created to demolish pork and greens?
Is there no *unfed* Hereafter, where the sound of chewing stops?
Is the atmosphere of heaven clammy with perpetual chops?
Do the friends of Mr Naylor sup on spirit-reared cow-heel?
Can the great Alexis Soyer really say 'Soyez tranquille?'
Or must I bring spirit beefsteak grilled in spirit regions hotter
For the spirit delectation of some spiritual squatter?
Shall I in a spirit kitchen hear the spirit blowflies humming,
Calming spiritual stomachs with a spiritual 'Coming!'?
Shall—but this is idle chatter, I have got my work to do.
'WAITER!' 'Yessir!' 'Wake up, stupid! Biled calves feet for
Number Two!'

W. T. Goodge

A Bad Break!

The preacher quoted, and the cranks
   Among his congregation smiled,
'How sharper than a serpent's thanks
   It is to have a toothless child.'

He saw he erred, his eye grew wild,
   He frowned upon the mirthful ranks:
'How toothless than a serpent's child
   It is to have a sharper's thanks!'

The M'Camley Mixture

Jack M'Camley
  Lank and long,
Ox-persuader,
  Billabong.
Bluff and hearty
  Sort o' party,
Got the 'bloody' habit strong.

Says the parson,
  Bright old bird,
'Why'd you use that
  Horrid word?—
(Jack looked grinful)—
  Not say sinful,
But most vulgar and absurd!'

'It's the bloody
  Church, betwixt
You and me, that
  Got me fixed!'
Says M'Camley,
  'In our fam'ly
Things is all so bloody mixed!

'There's me father—
  Whoa back, Dick!—
Church o' Bloody
  England, stric'!
There's me mother
  And one brother,
Roman—bloody—Catholic!

'But me sister—
  Way, you, Stan!
Don't them bullocks
  Rile a man?
Kilts enticed her,
  Went and spliced a
Presby—bloody—terian!'

A. B. Paterson

The Lost Leichhardt

'An English scientific society is fitting out a pioneering party to search for traces of the lost explorer Leichhardt.'

Another search for Leichhardt's tomb,
   Though fifty years have fled
Since Leichhardt vanished in the gloom,
   Our one Illustrious Dead!

But daring men from Britain's shore,
   The fearless bull-dog breed,
Renew the fearful task once more
   Determined to succeed.

Rash men, that know not what they seek,
   Will find their courage tried.
For things have changed on Cooper's Creek
   Since Ludwig Leichhardt died.

Along where Leichhardt journeyed slow
   And toiled and strayed in vain;
These rash excursionists must go
   Per Queensland Railway Train.

But on those deserts lone and drear
   The fierce Australian black
Will say, 'You show it pint o' beer,
   It show you Leichhardt's track!'

And loud from every squatter's door
   Each pioneering swell
Will hear the wild pianos roar
   The strains of 'Daisy Bell'.

The watchers in the forests vast
   Will see, at fall of night,
Commercial Travellers bounding past
   And darting out of sight.

About their path a fearful fate
   Will hover always near.
A dreadful scourge that lies in wait—
   The Longreach Horehound Beer!

And then, to crown this tale of guilt,
   They'll find some scurvy knave,
Regardless of their quest, has built
   A pub on Leichhardt's grave!

* * *

Ah yes! Those British pioneers
   Had best at home abide,
For things have changed in fifty years
   Since Ludwig Leichhardt died.

Henry Lawson

Rise Ye! Rise Ye!

Rise ye! rise ye! noble toilers! claim your rights with fire and steel!
Rise ye! for the cursed tyrants crush ye with the hiron 'eel!
They would treat ye worse than sla-a-aves! they would treat ye
        worse than brutes!
Rise and crush the selfish tyrants! ker-r-rush with your hobnailed
        boots!
  Rise ye! rise ye! glorious toilers!
  Rise ye! rise ye! noble toilers!
    Erwake! er-rise!

Rise ye! rise ye! noble toilers! tyrants come across the waves!
Will ye yield the Rights of Labour, will ye? *will* ye still be
        sla-a-aves?
Rise ye! rise ye! mighty toilers and revoke the rotten laws!
Lo, your wives go out a-washing while ye battle for the caws!
  Rise ye! rise ye! glorious toilers!
  Rise ye! rise ye! noble toilers!
    Erwake! er-rise!

Our gerlorious dawn is breaking! Lo, the tyrant trembles now!
He shall star-r-rve us here no longer! toilers will not bend or bow!
Rise ye! rise ye! noble toilers! Rise! behold, revenge is near;
See the Leaders of the People! Come an' 'ave a pint o' beer!
  Rise ye! rise ye! glorious toilers!
  Rise ye! rise ye! noble toilers!
    Erwake! er-rise!

Lo, the poor are starved, my brothers! Lo, our wives and children
        weep!
Lo, our women toil to keep us while the toilers are asleep!
Rise ye! rise ye! noble toilers! rise and break the tyrant's chain!
March ye! march ye! mighty toilers! even to the battle-plain!
  Rise ye! rise ye! glorious toilers!
  Rise ye! rise ye! noble toilers!
    Erwake! er-rrise!

E. G. Murphy ('Dryblower')

'Thank you, Mr Rason, for the Apples'

London item: 'At the Buckingham Palace banquet, given to the Colonial Premiers and others, Westralian apples were eaten by the King. He afterwards conversed with Westralia's Agent-General (C. H. Rason), and on parting said, "Thank you, Mr Rason, for the apples"'.

The banquet was a bonza, a rare recherche feed,
   Every item there was up-to-date and swagger,
From the appetizing oysters to the coffee and the weed,
   When the guests had waded through the Royal jagger.
There were squatters from the Sydneyside and butter kings from
      Vic.,
   Lack of space, alone, from naming them prevents us;
But the proudest pea of all who lapped the pale Imperial shick
   Was Rason, who in London represents us.
The King was kind and courteous, and had grins for every guest,
   With that tactfulness that always grips and grapples,
But to Hector's lug delighted came this message bright and blest—
   'Thank you, Mr Rason, for the apples!'

The assemblage was a brilliant one, for Deakin, silver-tongued,
   Had come to loose his oratory thrilling,
They hiccoughed Gord-Save-Edward with a chorus leather-lunged,
   What time the loyal liquor they were swilling.
They speeched of silver kinships, and of hands across the sea,
   They preached the same old platitudes redundant.
For whenever there's a plenitude of amber eau-de-vie,
   Cronk sentiment is equally abundant;
They boasted how the Empire's Sons would rally round the Flag,
   When Britain's drum reverberates and rapples,
But the ear of Cornthwaite Hector had no room for any gag
   Than 'Thank you, Mr Rason, for the apples!'

They were grown in boggy Boyanup, and washed by Darling dews,
   They were picked by cockies' kiddies fat and freckled,
Who little thought they'd ever mix with Nedward's banquet
      booze,
   When the Royal chef a score of flunkies heckled.
They were shipped aboard a liner with the butter and the beef,
   For weeks they heard the engine's diapason,

Till they reached where London's swindle-shark and market-
rigging thief
Rubs ribs with West Australia's only Rason.
They graced the Royal blow-out where the loyal speakers
wreathed,
His pappycock and persiflage and papples,
Till in Cornthwaite Hector's listener Ned the Seventh softly
breathed,
'Thank you, Mr Rason, for the apples.'

Little thought old sleepy Boyanup, of whom the world scarce
heard,
Where the poddy-calf pursues its mooing mummy,
That the product of its orchard would in London be interred
In a real, live, reigning, Royal Monarch's tummy,
Little thought the cockies' kiddies, who each morn the moo-cow
drain
Of milk that nearer blue than creamy-white is,
That the apples they'd exported would in time allay the pain
In a British Sovereign's paunch appendicitis,
Little thought they that an apple-core from Boyanup serene,
Might put Royalty to sleep in storied chapels,
Little thought our Agent-General would hear with blushing mien—
'Thank you, Mr Rason, for the apples!'

But supposing, just supposing, that the fruit from Boyanup
Upset the weak digestion of King Neddy,
Imagine how the household would be telephoning up
To get the surgeon's apparatus ready,
Imagine Alexandra mixing mustard in a pan
To put upon the Monarch's Little Mary,
Imagine how her feet would feel as round about she ran,
In a nightie rather delicate and airy;
It isn't very cosy to be wakened from a dream,
When the cold, grey dawn the Eastern darkness dapples,
While a King in fruit-convulsions mutters through the
poultice-steam—
'Blast you, Mr Rason, and your apples!'

John Shaw Neilson

The Case of Adam

There was a bold preacher named Campbell
Who said without any preamble
   There wasn't a fall
   There was no drop at all
I think the historians ramble.

Then the clerics who still had a calling
Declared this a thing most appalling
   But we'd better just say
   In a roundabout way
That it was a symbolical falling.

Whereupon an old party named Adam
Exclaimed to his wife, my dear Madam
   They have made a great fuss
   All along about us
But I think I may say that we've had 'em.

Norman Lindsay

The Penguin Bold

(From: *The Magic Pudding*)

To see the penguin out at sea,
   And watch how he behaves,
Would prove that penguins cannot be
   And never shall be slaves.
You haven't got a notion
How penguins brave the ocean,
   And laugh with scorn at waves.

To see the penguin at his ease
   Performing fearful larks
With stingarees of all degrees,
   As well as whales and sharks;
The sight would quickly let you know
The great contempt that penguins show
   For stingarees and sharks.

O see the penguin as he goes
   A-turning Catherine wheels,
Without repose upon the nose
   Of walruses and seals.
But bless your heart, a penguin feels
Supreme contempt for foolish seals,
   While he never fails, where'er he goes
   To turn back-flips on a walrus nose.

Lesbia Harford

Skirt Machinist

I am making great big skirts
For great big women—
Amazons who've fed and slept
Themselves inhuman.

Such long skirts, not less than two
And forty inches.
Thirty round the waist for fear
The webbing pinches.

There must be tremendous tucks
On those round bellies.
Underneath the limbs will shake
Like wine-soft jellies.

I am making such big skirts
And all so heavy,
I can see the wearers at
A lord-mayor's levee.

I, who am so small and weak
I have hardly grown,
Wish the skirts I'm making less
Unlike my own.

Leon Gellert

The Kangaroo

The very best Australian stew
always includes a kangaroo.
So if one happens to be shot,
just try it when you make a pot.
Lest you become a laughing-stock it
May be as well to search its pocket
For odds and ends that it may hold;—
Like lozenges (against a cold)—
Or rubber bands or bits of string—
Or bottle tops or anything
That filled the wretched creature's needs
From rolls of braid to coloured beads.
Such adjuncts (as the gourmet has it)
Possess no culinary asset.

The Mutton-Bird

Only a greenhorn (or a glutton)
Would seek the Mutton-bird for mutton.
For, be it known, he might as well
Pursue the Bellbird for a bell;
Or (passing on from brute to brute)
Approach the Fruitbat for some fruit;
Or (getting quite beyond control)
Track down the Polecat for a pole;
Which goes to prove our nomenclature
Is not in strict accord with Nature.

The Platypus

How gentle is the Platypus,
It neither growls nor makes a fuss,
But lies in its primeval ooze
And holds the most pacific views;
A loving creature, loved by all,
It never has been known to brawl;
Which may, or may not, be the roison
For its two glands of deadly poison.

John Goss

Williamanmary, the Cat

Though it strolls on the tiles with a swagger audacious,
And sits, like a judge, in our border herbaceous,
It sets us a problem to floor the sagacious
   Does Williamanmary, the cat.

Stretched out by the fire, it solemnly blinks there,
And looks like a sleek, shining, ebony sphinx there.
But whether a prince or a princess now winks there,
   Ask Williamanmary, the cat.

And whether it's masculine, feminine, neuter,
Whether she's suited or he is a suitor,
Is a point that's so moot that I know nothing mooter,
   Re Williamanmary, the cat.

But though it tenaciously makes no admissions,
I frankly confess I have got my suspicions,
That we'll soon be presented with pocket editions
   Of Williamanmary, the cat!

Fiat Justitia

When good King Alfred strung up forty judges,
He showed his subjects they should not forget
That there are ways to deal with legal smudges,
In short: Quis custodes custodiet?
When King Ahasuerus hanged judge Haman
Upon a gallows fifty cubits high,
He must have gratified the humblest layman
Who'd found that justice was too dear to buy.

But now we're told the law is just an ass;
At which the lawyer blandly smiles and whistles,
Content to let the innuendo pass
While browsing on his thousand-dollar thistles.
He knows the ones who ought to cry 'hee-haw'
Are all those donkeys who invoke the law.

Kenneth Slessor

Skis and Skies

I sing about Women and Winter,
  The rapture of 30 degrees,
The damsel who waits with a bundle of skates
  And the girl who goes riding on skis;
And, oh for the flight of an eagle
  To see where she happens to go—
But waving a wing is a difficult thing
  When you lie with your face in the snow.

Poo-pooh to your ice, Kosciusko,
  A fig for your cucumber air,
Your peaks, I'm informed, are sufficiently warmed
  By the presence of Annabel there;
But this I'm unable to warrant,
  The fact is, I really don't know—
Wherever I climb I spend most of my time
  With my face in a puddle of snow.

I know she has wings on her ankles,
  I know she can leap like a trout,
The hoi-polloi thrill when she whistles downhill
  And the guides find their eyes popping out;
For this I'll accept without question
  The word of the Tourist Bureau—
My personal view is a trifle askew
  Due to banging my face in the snow.

If only my skis wouldn't wobble,
  If only my feet would go straight,
I'd chase her with hope down a nursery slope
  And leave introductions to Fate;
But something has doomed me to grovel,
  I crawl on all fours down below,
She catapults by like a bird in the sky,
  And I lie with my face in the snow.

Eating by Yourself

Let aristocratic heroes
   Boast the platters of the Guelph,
You can dream of Trocaderos
   When you're dining by yourself;
You can hover like a glutton,
   You can order what you choose,
Try the fricassee of mutton,
   Toy with terrapin ragouts,
All the claret of Lugano,
   All the fairy teas-and-toasts,
Brought by Ferdinand Romano
   And a staff of lovely ghosts.

First the oysters, round and juicy,
   Served by some delightful girl—
Call her Nancy, call her Lucy,
   She may fetch perhaps a pearl;
Next the soup of tender turtle
   From a nymph with yellow hair—
Call her Mabel, call her Myrtle,
   She can spice it with a stare;
Then the fowl on gleaming china
   That a pretty creature brings—
Call her Dulcie, call her Dinah,
   You may find a pair of wings.

For a moment they will glimmer,
   For a twinkle they will gleam—
Then the kettle starts to simmer
   And they vanish like a dream;
You can whistle for them vainly,
   You may call in tender tones,
But the soup is printed plainly
   With the name of Foggitt, Jones;
Then you suddenly awaken—
   There's a sausage on the shelf,
And the bacon looks like bacon,
   And you're eating by yourself!

Robert D. FitzGerald

Favour

I'll not touch wood, nor, fingers crossed,
creep furtively for fear all's lost.
Luck's liquor pounding through the brain
I'll stand on kerbs and bellow
great news at my indifferent kin—
her favour towards this fellow.

Would you treat gently with that rowdy?
Flaunt or you flout her: Luck's no lady.
Yours in the lavish minute while
you take her gifts two-handed,
she'll break your heart for you, and smile,
so soon as she's so minded.

And pick your pocket when she goes . . .
But snap time's tail up: that hour's woes
will not snake round at now, bite back
where a game grip jerks a summons—
Luck loves him longest who can crack
this kind of lash on omens.

A. D. Hope

To Julia Walking Away

Darwin's daughters have no tails,
Yet a reminiscent motion
Agitates the lovely frails
At the seat of amputation.

Charles called Eve and Adam lies
And denied the garden state,
Yet the gait of Paradise
Could not wholly liquidate.

Julia's coccyx never can,
Swerving in delicious schism
Now to the Descent of Man,
Now towards Fundamentalism.

Darwin, Paley, from the dust
Argue in her ambulation:
Was Eve genuine, or just
A gorilla on probation?

The House of God

Morning service! parson preaches;
People all confess their sins;
God's domesticated creatures
Twine and rub against his shins;

Tails erect and whiskers pricking,
Sleeking down their Sunday fur,
Though demure, alive and kicking,
All in unison they purr:

'Lord we praise Thee; hear us Master!
Feed and comfort, stroke and bless!
And not too severely cast a
Glance upon our trespasses:

'Yesterday we were not able
To resist that piece of fish
Left upon the kitchen table
While You went to fetch the dish;

'Twice this week a scrap with Rover;
Once, at least, we missed a rat;
And we *do* regret, Jehovah,
Having kittens in Your hat!

'Sexual noises in the garden
Smelly patches in the hall—
Hear us, Lord, absolve and pardon;
We are humans after all!'

Home at last from work in Heaven,
This is all the rest God gets;
Gladly for one day in seven
He relaxes with His pets.

Looking down He smiles and ponders,
Thinks of something extra nice:
From His beard, O Joy, O wonders!
Falls a shower of little mice.

The Brides

Down the assembly line they roll and pass
Complete at last, a miracle of design;
Their chromium fenders, the unbreakable glass,
The fashionable curve, the air-flow line.

Grease to the elbows Mum and Dad enthuse,
Pocket their spanners and survey the bride;
Murmur: 'A sweet job! All she needs is juice!
Built for a life-time—sleek as a fish. Inside

'He will find every comfort: the full set
Of gadgets; knobs that answer to the touch
For light or music; a place for his cigarette;
Room for his knees; a honey of a clutch.'

Now slowly through the show-room's flattering glare
See her wheeled in to love, console, obey,
Shining and silent! Parson with a prayer
Blesses the number-plate, she rolls away

To write her numerals in his book of life;
And now, at last, stands on the open road,
Triumphant, perfect, every inch a wife,
While the corks pop, the flash-light bulbs explode.

Her heavenly bowser-boy assumes his seat;
She prints the soft dust with her brand-new treads,
Swings towards the future, purring with a sweet
Concatenation of the poppet heads.

Clover Honey

Father first noticed it: 'Upon my Sam,
This soil breeds spinsters! Five miles round, I swear,
Live twenty old maids—not that *I* give a damn,
But Mary and Susan here might have a care.

'Daughters are perishable goods at best;
At worst—Yes, dear, I *do* know when to stop—
But twelve at church today! Who would have guessed
So rich a shire could raise that blighted crop?'

Susan just giggled; I totted up father's count:
'Nineteen is what I make it, not twenty, Dad!'
'You've missed our gruesome help here, Sarah Blount,
Haven't you, girl? Admit it!'—and so I had.

'By God!'—he flourished his carvers in the air—
'She makes my flesh creep. No one asks *my* advice
Of course, but how your mother puts up with her
Passes my—yes, dear! yes, another slice?'

Susan and I discussed it later in bed.
'Father was horrid to laugh; he doesn't *know*!
If I don't marry,' said Sue, 'I'd rather be dead.'
I laughed too: 'Well, we've both some years to go.'

But for all that, I brooded on their lives;
Imagined them as young girls, like me or Sue;
Tried to imagine them happy mothers and wives
And wondered what went wrong—though mostly I knew.

Rumour, in country places, rarely leaves
Misfortune a shift or nakedness a clout.
At Tea-cup Time, when Gossip brings home her sheaves,
The skeletons rattle in closets for miles about.

Miss Tabitha and Miss Mildy at the Grange
Had been too high and mighty, people said;
Miss Prue had beauty, but no one thought it strange:
Papa had lost his money. The suitors fled.

Miss Martha had offers too. They had to wait—
A bed-ridden mother—and, as is often the case,
When free to marry, she found it was too late;
Miss Claire's club-foot cancelled that angel face.

Poor, gay Miss Belle never got her man to church;
There was Miss Madeleine, too—but never mind,
Too simple, too yielding: he left her in the lurch.
It's an old story, and people are so unkind.

Miss Sophie was unattractive from the start;
Miss Tetty, of course, had always been a shrew;
But why Miss Constance with her loving heart
Had never married, not even our gossips knew.

Eighteen is an uncompromising age.
Old maids, fag-ends of living, cat-fanciers,
I thought of them with mounting pity and rage
And blamed the order of the universe.

My father's friend,—he lived near us in Kent—
A Mr Darwin, used to visit our house
And when I raged at him in protest, sent
A twinkle at me from his beetle brows:

'Yes, yes, poor things!' he said, 'You have a heart
That does you credit, my dear. But let me say
That the great chain of being has found a part
In Nature's scheme even for them to play.

'You mentioned cats, I think. Each keeps a cat?'
'Good God!', I said, 'they have them by the score!'
'Indeed? Of course, I'm not surprised at that;
But cats catch mice—well, it's what cats are for.

'Their mistresses at night will put them out
To hunt for field-mice—you begin to see
My drift, perhaps, since as you know, no doubt,
The field-mouse preys upon the bumble-bee.

'These hirsute bees, and they alone, contrive
To fertilize the dark red-clover blooms;
Although it is their smaller cousins who hive
The clover-honey that loads our Kentish combs.

'So when we find—what does the Bible say?—
A land flowing with milk and honey, we do
Not doubt, we naturalists, that there we may
Expect to find old maids a-plenty too.

'The state of single blessedness, you see,
Is not without its talent; indeed, you might
Call spinsters partners of the honey bee
Bringer of life's best gifts, sweetness and light.'

Times change; old maids now in these parts are rare.
That would have made Mr Darwin smile, because
I hear old farmers in Kent here declare
The honey-flow is nothing like it was.

I did not marry, myself. As I recall
I have never had reason to complain of that.
Susan was wed, poor Sue, three times in all;
But now we live together. We keep a cat.

Ronald McCuaig

Pretty Kid

Framed by a plate of postered glass
She sits and sees the people pass
Through eyes that, great and golden brown,
Roll into joy the visible town;
But her young breasts comprise her main
Business asset; of these you gain
A private view when, bending bare
Of any restrictive underwear,
She fiddles about and hesitates
Deep in her pile of cigarettes:
And lonely smokers, blowing rings,
Dream that they see those exquisite things
Dangling desire from wavering wreaths,
Which soon more sage reflection breathes
Away with hope; that base emotion
Ever should trade on sales-promotion
No good customer dares expect;
One feels it would not seem correct;
Besides, her husband might object.

The Letter

Dear, as I write and think of you,
And several other people too,
The flooring of the flat above,
Creaking with aged, illicit love,
Reminds me, when I was trying to write
These very words the other night,
He spoke from three till half past four
Merely repeating she was a whore;
The boy below has just begun
To find it not precisely fun;
The trouble is, as he explained
The Thursday evening when it rained
To a judicial prig of a friend
(I thought their talk would never end)
The girl is really not the kind
Of girl he really had in mind;
But still he keeps her on, for fear
Of hurting her; and now I hear
The lovely girl who loves to dwell,
And dwells to love, across the well,
Saying, since he is married, he
Should be considerate, in that she
Is taking risks; as for the rent,
She fears, it has been otherwise spent;
The opposite flat is dark and dumb,
Yet I feel certain he will come
Home to his love as drunk as ever,
And, in a slowly rising fever,
Noting the whiskey bottle gone,
Will trip and curse and stumble on
Into the bathroom; pull the chain;
Fumble the cabinet; curse again;
Will ask the slut where she has hid
His toothbrush; blunder back to bed;
Find his pyjamas tied in knots
And give her, as he puts it, what's
Coming to her; she won't escape
Her deeply meditated rape;
But I must write of love, and all
That once was high and had a fall,
And how I burn; and I confess

It gives me little happiness:
Encompassed so, my rooms become
A kind of lovers' vacuum,
Dear, as I write, and ache for you,
And dream of all that we could do
If these delights thy mind might move
To live with me and be my love.

Hector Monro

You'll Love Their Fubsy, Tangy Charm

They hammer us with glamour as they clamour to enamour us,
The barrel-breasted beauties of the television screen.
So slim and trim and lithe of limb for all they're hyper-mammarous,
They shatter our resistance to the utmost smithereen.

It's credible they're edible. Or beddable? Unspreadable
That titillating rumour must remain*
A complex which deflects their sex has made that path untreadable,
As I shall now endeavour to explain.

Though the splendour that they tender has indubitable gender
And their object's to enrapture and inflame,
No sweet conceit makes them compete for masculine surrender
And it's not their own attractions they proclaim.

Their enticing has its pricing but they're so self-sacrificing
That they channel the enchantment of their swains
From lips and eyes and hips and thighs for paradise sufficing
To the stuff you use for cleaning out the drains.

Though created to be mated they are so infatuated
With deodorants, depilatories and soap,
With food that you'd have thought eschewed by palates cultivated,
That it's only with detergents they'll elope.

---

* Our tribal laws of libel in a labyrinth unthreadable
Will trap us if the sponsors should complain.

Faith Before Birth

'Monash males have been asked to donate sperm to a research and artificial insemination project being carried out by the Monash department of obstetrics and gynaecology at Queen Victoria Medical Centre . . . To enable parents to have a child with traits similar to their own, donors are computer matched with the husband's physical characteristics, race and religion.' *Monash Reporter* March 1978

The infant, though not yet conceived,
Has pondered, doubted and believed.
(Its credo, as a minimum,
Acknowledges a Life to Come,
Nor can it readily forsake a
Suspicion that it has a Maker.)
And so the thoughtful medico,
God's understudy here below,
Forestalling any future schism,
Will hear the sperm its catechism,
For if by probing he should find
It atheistically inclined
He knows that it would ill behove him
To fertilise a pious ovum.

Fundamentalist

From: *A Short Guide to Religion*

Fifteenth Chapter of Isaiah
Proves the Pope to be a liar.
Joshua XVI: 57
Shows that good men go to Heaven;
Deuteronomy XII and 3
Proves that this applies to me;
Genesis XI: 2
That it is not meant for you.

Modernist

From: *A Short Guide to Religion*

We've amazing breadth of mind,
We are tolerant and kind,
We'll consider any view you care to name.
We're not sure that God exists,
But our piety persists,
And we tolerantly worship just the same.

We're not certain we believe
In Adam or in Eve,
For Jonah we've the frigidest of glances,
We do not care at all
For the doctrines of Saint Paul,
But we're always moved to rapture by Saint Francis.

* * *

Matthew, Mark, Luke and John
Bless the faith that we stand on;
But we must confess we're not sure
How to work in Job and Joshua!

The Mystic East

From: *A Short Guide to Religion*

Oozy Woozy Goo
Is the Way of Life for You!
Oozy! Woozy! Oozy Woozy Goo!
Oozy Woozy is the Inner Light,
The Perfect Non-attachment of the Infinite!
The Esoteric Mysteries of the Threefold Way,
The Mystical Vibrations of the Psychic Ray,
The You-in-Me and the Me-in-You,
Oozy! Woozy! Oozy Woozy Goo!

Thought is eternal! Thought's divine!
But of course they must be Thoughts like mine.
Thoughts of Perfection, Thoughts of Love,
Thoughts of the Olive Branch and Dove,
Thoughts of Purity Within,
But mostly the Thought of the Vitamin:
Thoughts of Carrot-and-Seaweed Stew.
Oozy! Woozy! Oozy Woozy Goo!

Aristotle

From: *The Sonneteer's History of Philosophy*

When Aristotle, Alexander's tutor,
Was asked by that young sprig to tell him how
He could secure more laurels for his brow,
The sage, forgetting that he just meant loot, or
More probably, believing it astuter
Not to indulge an impulse to avow
That all his pupil's conduct up to now
Revealed the morals of a barracouta
And that the Form imposed upon his Matter,
The Soul, the Essence or the Actuality
Arising out of his Potentiality,
Would lead him on to murder, rape and batter,
Returned this answer to the age-old riddle:
'Gold be thy mean, distributed thy middle.'

Karl Marx

From: *The Sonneteer's History of Philosophy*

Karl Marx, like Job, was suffering from boils
When he divined, within that Reading Room
Now dubbed the British Library, the doom
Of every class except the one that toils.
To say much more than that at once embroils
The chronicler in trying to say whom
His mantle landed on. I'll not presume,
But just remark, as they dispute the spoils,
Perhaps it was not wholly persiflage
That prompted Karl one morning to exclaim
'I am no Marxist'. Not to him the blame
For all the crimes committed in his name.
Others, not he, must answer Milton's charge:
New Commissar is but old Czar writ large.

Bertrand Russell

From: *The Sonneteer's History of Philosophy*

It seemed to Russell, as to Socrates,
To be the merest, dullest common sense
That one should base beliefs on evidence.
And, indeed, the precept seemed to please
When he applied it to geometries,
To working out which logic represents
This world of ours and all its complements
And other abstract problems such as these.
But when he tried to live by it as well
He found himself inside a prison cell.
For mixing logic up with War or Marriage
Is something all right-minded men disparage.
The life of reason's positively treasonable
When no one else is willing to be reasonable.

John Bray

The Birds on North Terrace

How odd in this most staid of cities
Appear these twittering committees,
Passing with choric epithet
The motion that the sun now set.
They counterpoint with trills and shakes
The rasp of tyres and shriek of brakes,
Impervious to blackball or snub,
They serenade the Adelaide Club,
And from aloft their dropping star
Mercedes Benz and Jaguar,
Postscripting with earth's commentary
The affluent society.

St George and the Dragon Discussion Group

As the young man chafing in armour off the peg
Jogtrotted down the Lydda highway on his hack,
Newly acquired from Ares' used horse mart,
Fumbling the stiff scabbard and trying to remember
All the demonstrations in the nightschool on spearcraft,
There accosted him a clutch of learned persons
From various faculties, who thus addressed him.

'Wait till all the facts are in. Every question
Is multilateral. You are overlooking
The dragon's viewpoint. Non-intervention
Is your only duty, till a commission,
To be appointed in twenty-seven days
By an international body, has reported.'

'Dragons are symptoms. They will continue
Till we have socialism. Tilting at dragons
Is mere adventurism. Read Marx on Monsters.'

'There is no monster. Advertising agents,
Pushing the tourist trade, plus ancestral memories
Of the myth of Perseus promote mass hysteria.'

'Young man, these fantasies of dragon-slaying
And princess-rescuing appear psychotic.
They are both signs of immaturity
And maladjustment to your peer group
With whom you should be home competing now
In business, sport, or buying on instalments
A family chariot to take out driving
Your statistical one point seven children.'

'Dragons come from Tartary. Now we have the one.
If he is injured the Grand Cham will avenge him.
We will be invaded by a horde of basilisks,
Cockatrices, mantichores, asps and amphisboenas.
Great sea-serpents will coil along the coastline,
Flailing down the shipping and fissioning the waterfronts.
One princess yearly we find expendable.
Do you want forty virgins crunched a fortnight?'

St George turned homeward, somewhat disconsolate,
And took up a career in public relations.

Non Event

Let's agree to sever,
Saving grief and gloom.
You want a freehold property.
I want a motel room.

Better abort the friendship
Before it's too old to kill.
You want a Joan and Darby.
I want a Fanny Hill.

We would never have been concordant,
Either in heart or head.
You want a lifelong union.
I want an hour in bed.

You can't say I deceived you.
I never promised rings.
You want Tristan and Isolde.
I want a twang on the strings.

Dilemma

I have inherited eight chairs,
Straight-backed Victorian affairs,
Leather, and stuffed with equine hairs,
Plucked from the manes of Arab mares,
In days of bustles, chignons, squares,
Disraeli bought the Suez shares,
Ladies in carriages and pairs
Drove to inspect the tradesman's wares,
My grandmother purchased these chairs.
Now they are slashed with rents and tears,
The springs stick out like Gorgons' hairs,
They are turned into risks and snares
To trap the sitters' derrieres
And hurl them groundwards unawares.
The cost to make needful repairs
Would, the upholsterer declares,
Suffice to pave the Golden Stairs,
Then last for sixty years, he swears.
Should I submit? What poet cares
To paste good money on old chairs
To pad the arses of his heirs?

Entomology and Below

The insect world and I can symbiose,
Each thing that flies or flaps or creeps or blows:
Those that molest me with a sigh I kill.
Collectively I bear them no ill will.

Bacteria also I can recognise.
They move and eat and breed and socialise.
Anti-biotics knock the bad ones flat.
The good ones get some All Bran and a pat.

The virus, though, bears no responsive trait.
No lens can track it and no filter stay.
Like a miasma or a vagrant ghost,
It comes from nowhere and befouls its host.

The chest and nostrils strive and heave and drudge,
Clogged with obscene and sluggish swamps of sludge.
Eve would have dropped the apple from her hold,
Had she foreseen it cloned the common cold.

Barbara Giles

Pretty Ditty

The spring, the spring, the joyful spring,
the rooting pig shall wear a ring.
The fields are green, the grass grows quick,
as does the incubated chick.
The new leaves on the willows quiver,
the force-fed goose enlarges liver.
All the birds have come again,
blessed be the stayput battery hen.
Thick on the flats the lucerne grows
to feed the stalled and munching cows.
Unkindly altered little ram
grows placidly to best spring lamb.
And plants, to feed the money vultures,
are hot-house raised from tissue cultures.
We, pent and treadmilled in our cages,
while balmy-aired the green spring rages,
proliferate black marks on pages.

O Oedipus! O Mores!

Innocent infant, sucking your thumb,
for you the explanation's all to come.
Addict of oral, anal satisfaction,
you don't relate as yet to other action
when all that's hollow, round, or long erect
must be discussed in manner circumspect,
lest your most innocent and artless tricks
should be considered as erotic fix.
Significant all play with bats and balls,
while boys build towers, girls build enclosing walls.
Once and forever proved by Oedipus,
the love of parents is incestuous,
though you seem happy blowing bubbles, dribbling,
you're ripening a hatred for a sibling.
Conflict of id and Ego will appal you,
castration fears, or penis envy gall you.
The Freudian stew is bubbling, rich and gluey.
Don't worry, darling, most of it is hooey.

To All Hereditary Princes

Spawned like a plebeian, where's your cause for pride?
mere sum of Adam's rage to procreate.
The covetous seed will cleave what chance provide
genes random pairing randomly decide
the endowments of a future head of state.

And there you are. The eagle nose of Rome,
your father's dullness, mother's complexion maybe.
But just as possibly an errant chromosome
will bring you forth a hunchback little gnome,
devious, brilliant, princedom's parody.

And all the vigilance, and all the bars
that hedge a queen, have not made princes certain
their own emissaries in the skirmish are
the only entries. Was the door ajar?
Is there a commoner behind the curtain?

John Blight

The Glove

Thrown in—a glove! full dress for a
softer generation when wool and
wheat were not burdensome to
the merchants, but commodities
with which the teams shouldered the loads
across plains and over mountains.

Soft dress, warm-hearted drapery
carried as accessories at
Christmas even in the roasting
weather of garden parties, with
frail fans wielded as gestures to
the heat.

My sisters, you have thrown
such lumber into discard. The
'glove thrown in' as signal of defeat!
or 'down' as challenge? Which is the
mode of your undress?

I recall
the dove-like apparel of young
ladies, in my youth. Better I
had not found this grey mimicry
from a past when burning its waste.

Dorothy Auchterlonie

Insomniacs, Please Note

(The Prime Minister, Mr McMahon, said last night that when he was unable to sleep he turned to the Bible to help him get 6 or 7 hours rest—News item, 24 April 1972)

Which portion does he read when sleep eludes him?
If only he had told reporters that!
Zephaniah 3 or *Micah* 2, or
8 *Chronicles* where 'Benjamin begat . . .'?

Lamentations 5 is too disturbing,
Hosea 8 is rather more than that;
Joel 1 is frankly quite perturbing,
It must be *Chronicles*, where 'Kish begat . . .'

The 'Sermon on the Mount' would hardly soothe him,
And *Matthew* 25 would raise a doubt
About his status as a sheep or goat, and
His sleep would vanish while he worked it out.

Acts 4, verse 31-to-5 is hopeless,
The Party would be wondering what he's at;
And *Romans* 12 is equally seditious—
Safer with *Chronicles* where 'Ram begat . . .'

Numbers 26 might also serve him,
And *Joshua* 12 is reasonably flat;
But *Deuteronomy* has hidden treasures—
He'd best rely on 'Ahitub begat . . .'

(Selah) To use the Word of God as soporific
Would seem a rather blasphemous mistake:
Let's hope that soon the Lord will rise and smite him
With a passage that will shock him wide awake.

David Campbell

Small-Town Gladys

There are rows of bottles against the glass;
I look between and my hair's blonde grass,
My lips are berries and my skin is cream
And I fill my frock to the very brim
And twirl a curl when the sportsmen pass—
And I'm a good girl, I am.

They call me Glad and say I'm a queen.
I look in the glass and my eyes are green
And they talk to men though they make no sound
For it's love that makes the world go round;
But go too far and I say, 'Go on;
I am a good girl, I am.'

In every novel I'm Lady Jane,
I use the book as a wicked fan,
And I sit on a stool and my fingers knit
A web to snare a sportsman's wit;
And they look at me as they look for rain,
But I'm a good girl, I am.

Under the willows, under the night,
Where schoolboys spy and the parson might,
I am the moon that rules the tides
Of men. And I shake and hold my sides
And I say, 'My make-up's an awful sight—
And I'm a good girl, I am.'

Jack Spring

The day the back lavatory
Went down the creek,
Boys looked from the orchard
And up strode Jack.

'There's ten bob in silver
For the first son of mine
To own that he pushed it
And speak like a man.'

'Father, I did it.
I only meant
To ease her a little
And in she went.

'That's ten bob, father.'
'Now hear me, son:
I've five white florins
For Washington

'And the father of a hiding
Unless you prove to me
The father of George Washington
Was in the cherry-tree.'

The Australian Dream

The doorbell buzzed. It was past three o'clock.
The steeple of St Andrew's weathercock
Cried silently to darkness, and my head
Was bronze with claret as I rolled from bed
To ricochet from furniture. Light! Light
Blinded the stairs, the hatstand sprang upright,
I fumbled with the lock, and on the porch
Stood the Royal Family with a wavering torch.

'We hope,' the Queen said, 'we do not intrude.
The pubs were full, most of our subjects rude.
We came before our time. It seems the Queen's
Command brings only "Tell the dead marines!"
We've come to you.' I must admit I'd half
Expected just this visit. With a laugh
That put them at their ease, I bowed my head.
'Your Majesty is most welcome here,' I said.
'My home is yours. There is a little bed
Downstairs, a boiler-room, might suit the Duke.'
He thanked me gravely for it and he took
Himself off with a wave, 'Then the Queen Mother?
She'd best bed down with you. There is no other
But my wide bed. I'll curl up in a chair.'
The Queen looked thoughtful. She brushed out her hair
And folded up *The Garter* on a pouf.
'Distress was the first commoner, and as proof
That queens bow to the times,' she said, 'we three
Shall share the double bed. Please follow me.'

I waited for the ladies to undress—
A sense of fitness, even in distress,
Is always with me. They had tucked away
Their state robes in the lowboy; gold crowns lay
Upon the bedside tables; ropes of pearls
Lassoed the plastic lampshade; their soft curls
Were spread out on the pillows and they smiled.
'Hop in,' said the Queen Mother. In I piled
Between them to lie like a stick of wood.
I couldn't find a thing to say. My blood
Beat, but like rollers at the ebb of tide.
'I hope your Majesties sleep well,' I lied.
A hand touched mine and the Queen said, 'I am
Most grateful to you, Jock. Please call me Ma'am.'

The Tourist Trade

Where once the ghostly swagman,
As curlews haunt a swamp,
Cried, 'Who'll come waltz Matilda?'
They've built a tourist camp.

Cod flap among detergents,
Refusing lemonade
And sing with tenor voices,
God bless the tourist trade!

The wallabies are busy
Hopping from His to Hers
And stuff their Fowler toilets
Brimful with Bathurst burrs;

Then stand with young in pouches
To see the tourists pass
Like Swan Lake ballerinas
With thistles up their arse.

At dusk the last koala
Hands out an ice grenade
To Mum & Dad & Kevin
To spread the tourist trade.

Canberra Incident

At the Treasury the girls were making tea
While we made love. While we were making love
They walled the valley; water greened above
Us locked like bees in summer amber. We
Are the true guardians of this garden city
Who died as lovers die that it might live
And fertilized by us, each morning give
Thanks over teacups at the Treasury.

The horned god passed. Young women dressed in denim,
In faunskin, ran with song and willow wands
To the thin woods about Mount Ainslie. There
They danced a measure, plaiting in their hair
Snakes and wild orchid, and hunting down like hounds
The Treasurer, they tore him limb from limb.

Mothers and Daughters

The cruel girls we loved
Are over forty,
Their subtle daughters
Have stolen their beauty;

And with a blue stare
Of cool surprise,
They mock their anxious mothers
With their mothers' eyes.

John Manifold

The Sirens

Odysseus heard the sirens; they were singing
Music by Wolf and Weinberger and Morley
About a region where the swans go winging,
Vines are in colour, girls are growing surely

Into nubility, and pylons bringing
Leisure and power to farms that live securely
Without a landlord. Still, his eyes were stinging
With salt and sea blink, and the ropes hurt solely.

Odysseus saw the sirens; they were charming,
Blonde, with snub breasts and little neat posteriors,
But could not take his mind off the alarming

Weather report, his mutineers in irons,
The radio failing; it was bloody serious.
In twenty minutes he forgot the sirens.

Chillianwallah Station

When his hopes of a colonelcy faded away
He retired to the colonies, still on half-pay,
Preferring to Cheltenham a Gulf-country run
And a heat of a hundred-and-ten in the sun.

His cook was a Cantonese—Asian at least!—
Who thought enough curry as good as a feast;
And his ex-soldier servant, from Antrim, named Barney,
Used to rowse the black stockmen in bad Hindustani.

He kept the fair flag of the Empire afloat
By wearing a tunic done up to the throat;
And the style of his most conversational speeches
Had its thumbs well in line with the seam of its breeches.

He played a straight bat, and a good hand at solo,
He would ride forty miles for a chukker of polo,
So the district forgave him his finical pride
Which demurred for so long at selecting a bride.

Then the seasons got worse, and the banks took a hand,
They called in the mortgage they held on his land;
And the Major was found in the harness-room, shot
Thro' the head with his old-fashioned Webley-&-Scott.

The jury said: 'Accident; no one's to blame;'
And the Major was buried, leaving only the name
'Chillianwallah' in letters some eight inches high
On the gate at the stock-route to remember him by.

Except that old Barney's the grandfather now
Of a quarter-caste family, no one knows how,
Who have never been coached since the Major passed on,
But who ride like the Ashtons and bat like the Don.

Outer Suburbs

It seems you can't have gracious living and
Goannas. Shiny villas multiply
On what were quite attractive bits of land,
And we'll be getting sewerage by and by.

Down where Macpherson's smithy used to stand
They've built a supermarket on the sly.
'It's progress', says my neighbour; 'Things expand.'
But living creatures are in short supply.

We haven't had goannas in the yard
For six or seven years. They were the first
To leave, and then the frillies. That was hard.

The only newcomers are oversexed
Damned greedy sparrows, breeding fit to burst.
They drove the wrens away. It's our turn next.

Musicians

Musicians, who at will have otherwhere
To be, turn up in unexpected places.
Rapt in the overture to *Le Corsaire*
They are, and are not, at the local races.

While gangsters wreck a joint, its jazzmen blare
Unintermittently with in-turned faces,
And at King Louis' elbow stands a pair
Of—nobles? Bishops? No, of double-basses.

Doomsday. The heavens are shrivelled, earth is torn.
Now, smartly, goats to this side, sheep to that!
Millions of sinners wail in hell, forlorn.

Smug saints applaud God's sense of tit-for-tat.
Gabriel stands apart, and sucks his horn
Morosely, brooding on his last B-flat.

Judith Wright

The True Religion

'The industry's a clean one,'
The Pious Miner said,
'No fumes, no smell, no garbage;
just a clean sweep instead.
We'll take your useless wastelands,
fit only now for ducks;
trade no-cost roads and powerlines
for fifty million bucks.

'For aeons they've existed
and never earned a cent,
but now we have the know-how
to use them as God meant.
Come all ye pious miners,
with dozer and with dredge;
we'll tidy up the country,
we promise and we pledge.

'You Extreme Nature-lover,
we cannot understand
your Substitute Religion
that's built upon the sand.
Ours is the True Religion.
Our glorious Company
will bring you all the blessings
of our technology.

'Your Reverence for Nature
is obviously fake.
It never made a dollar,
while look at what we make!
The Good Works to our credit
stand as the angels bright
and show that Heaven chose us
to prove the Miner's Right.'

The Extreme Nature-lover
stood weeping on the sands
watching the Last of Dollars
torn from the Last of Lands.
'Come, dry those tears,' they told him.
'Why mourn the simpler creatures?
The Economic Landscape
has more attractive features.'

The No-Cost Roads, the Powerlines,
the Parks for Recreation
spread far and wide their glories
to benefit the nation.
The rows of casuarinas
that whimpered as they grew
proved that the great RZDA*
respected nature too.

The Economic Landscape
lay bare, eroded, still,
while every Mines Department
exclaimed ''Tis Heaven's will!'
The view of poets packing
and artists taking wing
increased their satisfaction.
'Gone—and a damn good thing!

'This is the You Beaut Country,
so quality-controlled,
with not a dune or forest
that can't be bought or sold.
Their substitute religion
(sincere, we hardly doubt)
was primitive, though blissful.
We're better off without.'

So to the True Religion
each acre was converted,
and every bird or poet
departed or deported,
while safe at last for progress
and great RZDA
and drained of every dollar
the happy landscape lay.

'Twas not the land they wept for.
They loved not our society;
they worshipped false divinities.
Ours is the truer piety.
So join our congregation;
Australia is our pigeon.
Raise high the hymn to Camm and Sim:
"The Buck's the True Religion".'

---

* Rutile and Zircon Development Association

James McAuley

Jindyworobaksheesh

By the waters of Babylon
I heard a Public Works official say:
'A culture that is truly Babylonian
Has been ordered for delivery today.'

By the waters of Babylon
A quiet noise of subsidies in motion.
'To a bald or mangy surface we apply
Our sovereign art-provoking lotion.'

By the waters of Babylon I heard
That art was for the people; but they meant
That art should sweeten to the people's mouth
The droppings from the perch of government.

The True Discovery of Australia

Erret, et extremos alter scrutetur Iberos

* * *

Let them wander and scrutinize the outlandish Australians

(Thoreau)

Willem Janszoon may well have been the first
To leave a bootprint on our shore, but he
Disqualified himself by being Dutch
From celebration in our history.

Dampier, that cool observant pirate,
Could fill an epic, and deserve the fuss;
But he, it seems, preferred the Hodmadods
And said that they were gentlemen to us.

Others, too, line up for epic treatment,
Discoverers of river-mouths and harbours;
But they must take their turn, as mortals do,
Who wait in beauty-salons or the barber's.

The one who now receives attention is,
Beyond all doubt, our True Discoverer,
Though verse has hitherto ignored his claim:
The glorious and forgotten Gulliver,

Who found his Lilliput where you will find
Lilliput still, and more so than before:
Close to Lake Torrens by his reckoning,
Though it has since expanded more and more

Till now the population maps display
An acne rash, disfiguring the whole rind
Of white Australia, as she hugely squats
Above her pint-pot, flyblown and resigned.

And whereas Gulliver has been neglected,
Hushed up almost, as of bad repute,
I here propose that we should change the name
Of Yorke Peninsula to Gulliver's Boot.

(For the benefit of readers overseas,
Not the steeple rising to a height
On pious Queensland, but the curious leg
That paddles in the south just near the Bight.)

Since it is usual in histories
To make a contribution to research
By adding some new evidence or other,
I felt that Swift had left me in the lurch

By writing everything that could be known
About the great sea-captain; but I went
To Ida Leeson at the Mitchell, saying:
'I don't suppose you have a document . . .'

Of course she had one! Had it there for years.
Near 'Phar Lap (See Houyhnhnms)' on the shelf:
A letter written to Lord Peterborough
And signed by honest Lemuel himself

In 1729; wherein he gives
The noble lord some further reasons why
He deprecates a recent move to float
A Lilliput Investment Company.

'The place, my lord, is much like Gideon's fleece
The second time he laid it on the ground;
For by the will of God it has remained
Bone-dry itself, with water all around.

'Yet, as a wheel that's driven in the ruts,
It has a wet rim where the people clot
Like mud; and though they praise the inner spaces,
When asked to go themselves, they'd rather not.

'The men are brave, contentious, ignorant;
The women very much as one expects.
For their religion, I must be excused,
Having no stomach to observe their sects.

'You must be wary in your conversation;
For, seeing them thumb-high, you might suppose
They recognised their stature, but beware!
Their notion of themselves is grandiose.

'And you will often find, although their heads
Are like a berry on a twig of bones,
They speak as giants of the South Pacific
And treat the islands as their stepping-stones.

'North-east across the water, Brobdingnag
Casts its momentous shadow on the sea
And fills the sky with thunder; but they smile
And sit on their verandahs taking tea,

'Watching through the pleasant afternoons
Flood, fire and cyclone in successive motion
Complete the work the pioneers began
Of shifting all the soil into the ocean.

'Sometimes they have to light the lamps at noon,
And seal their houses that are shipping dust
Like vessels in a storm; and truth to say
It is a kind of shipwreck. But they trust

'In providence: the Almighty's, not their own.
Meanwhile, as you'd expect, their arts are poor
As if the dust had leaked into their brains
And made a kind of dry-rot at the core.

'Knowledge is regarded with suspicion.
Culture to them is a policeman's beat;
Who, having learnt to bully honest whores,
Is let out on the Muses for a treat.

'Their Addison, their Swift, 's a magistrate.
Matters of aesthetics courts determine.
Detectives play Petronius Arbiter
And hunt the poetasters down like vermin.

'The citizenry takes no part. For it,
Plato's a horse, Socrates a dog.
Surrounded by its vast domains, it sleeps:
A pigmy in the iron bed of Og.

'In prehistoric times the land was flat;
But then the mobile flange along the east
Buckled against the stubborn central shield,
Whereby a lowly mountain-range was creased.

'Mentally, they're still in Pliocene,
A flat terrain impermeably dense;
And will be so, until volcanic mind
Arches its back at brute indifference.

'The Southern Sea, my lord, in time to come
Will be the Bargain Basement of the earth,
With nations like demented women snatching
Remnants without inquiring what they're worth.

'Britannia may find herself obliged
To put a lot of oddments on the docket.
But you yourself, my lord, I should advise
To keep your money in your breeches' pocket.

'Your most obedient, L. Gulliver.'
Also, as Appendix B, I add
A recent find: a manuscript containing
Rejected verses of the Dunciad.

(Can this hard-mouthed, four-legged stanza trot
At such a stylish pace? I dare say not.
Yet here I make my verse a heliotrope,
Obsequiously proud, and follow Pope.)

'Let Fame's posterior trumpet sound once more!
Booksellers, make obeisance; bards, adore!
The King of Crambo, daubed with paint and smut,
A giant Nothing, comes to Lilliput.

'Th'egregious penguin, amorously blind,
Confuses oft a man with penguin-kind;
And at his feet, for reasons of its own,
Deposits, with quaint gravity, a stone.

'Less wonder, then, if now the silly bird,
By its own likeness gulled, adores th'absurd.
The huge Decoy inspires a solemn fuss
And to the tribe becomes eponymous.

'For lucid Ern, ye penguins, weep no more:
Henceforth he is the genius of the shore.
If, unawares, you stumble into sense,
His arm shall save, and your own impudence.

'Where'er th'Antarctic surge . . .' But here a mouse
Has put his tooth to the historic scribble.
Would there had been a Vegetative Eye,
Or piece of Bread and Cheese, for him to nibble!

And with the mouse, my modest epic ends.
Gulliver refurbished takes the air.
Calliope, indifferent, says 'Who's next?'
And waves a customer into the chair.

But while the girl's not looking, I shall add
A private Envoi or reflective Coda
To readers fit though few: in a country where
An acorn-cup would seem a scotch-and-soda,

A man of even middling parts will look
So tall, he may forget his real status,
And play the sorry fable of the frog
Who burst his belly with his own afflatus.

The Convict and the Lady

An incident in St George's Church, Battery Point

Voluntaries of Clarke and Boyce
  Flow temperately sweet
With Gamba, Flute and Clarabel,
And pedal Bourdon trampled well
  By shapely kid-skinned feet.

An apparition from the tower
  Suspends the diapason.
Will she scream? No, courage wins,
And in that empty church begins
  An interesting liaison.

'Lady, I am a fugitive
  That's taken refuge here.
Up into the tower I crept,
Two days and nights I've waked and slept,
  But hunger masters fear.

'Now fetch me food, or fetch the law,
  For I am at your mercy.
Though forfeited in youthful spleen,
My birth and station were not mean,
  My name is Eustace Percy.'

So every day she brings her lunch,
  And practises the organ.
She finds him breeches, coat and vest,
And takes word to The Sailor's Rest,
  To a man named Harry Morgan.

One Sunday, as the lady plays
  'Recessional in A',
A stranger joins the genteel throng
That files out after Evensong;
  Unmarked, he slips away.

In darkness a small boat rows out
  Into the estuary.
The brig looms up upon the tide,
A shadow clambers up the side—
  And Eustace Percy's free!

So ends the tale? No, three years passed;
   From Hull a letter came:
'I thrive in my new way of life . . .'
The lady sailed to be his wife,
   And shared a borrowed name.

Organist, for that lady's sake,
   Select your stops and play
This postlude that I chose expressly,
By Samuel Sebastian Wesley,
   'Recessional in A'.

Tabletalk

In tabletalk my father used to tell
Of the escaped nun kidnapped by a priest;
Or innocent girls in the confessional,
Closeted in the dark with some gross beast.

By contrast, Anglican restraint was good:
It kept religion in its proper place.—
What all this talk was for, I understood
Only long after; but it left a trace.

In an unguarded moment once, I drew
Deserved rebuke for letting on I had
A plan of reading the whole Bible through:
He thought this a quick way of going mad.

On relatives my parents were agreed:
Too much association doesn't do,
And doubly so with the bog-Irish breed—
They're likely to want something out of you.

On friendship too the doctrine was as cold:
They're only making use of you you'll find;
Prudence consists in learning to withhold
The natural impulse of the sharing mind.

What is the wisdom that a child needs most?
Ours was distrust, a coating behind the eye
We took in daily with the mutton roast,
The corned beef salad, and the shepherd's pie.

Rosemary Dobson

Piltdown Man

Piltdown Man is shelved away
Piltdown Man has had his day,
nine split fragments joined in one,
parietal pieces of cranium.
All to himself in the British Museum
Piltdown Man is singing this song:

'Mandible, canine, turbinal,
stegodon, flint, and broken skull,
we all lay low in a gravel-bed—
if there ever was a body it lost its head.

'They found us out and they joined us up,
pieced my skull like a broken cup;
eminent men in the lecture room
threw up their hats when I came in.

'Prolonged applause for antiquity,
stamping feet for stratigraphy—
I held the stage but it didn't last long:
fluorine tests have done me wrong.

'Radio counts that showed excess,
spectrographic analysis—
applications of science proved
Piltdown Man has never lived.'

Piltdown Man is quite disproved.
He never lived and he never loved.
A gravel-bed's a private place—
but whom (and what with) to embrace?
Oh listen hard and listen long
for the sad lost notes of the Piltdown song.

Oracles for a Childhood Journey

The painted billboards spoke to me.
Out of the Blue Comes the Whitest Wash
and *Doctor Morse's Indian Root*
(They Reach the Liver) Pills,
reiterated loud and strong
all the way to Mittagong.

I put the question from the train
all the way to Mittagong,
What does the future hold for me?
Not Pythian Snakes nor Sacred Bough
gave answers more oracularly—
Doctor Morses's Indian . . . Rea . . .

All the way to Mittagong
I asked of flying cloud and sky,
And shall I then write Poetry?
And whence shall come the words to me?
And whence the masks to speak them through?
Out of the Blue, Out of the Blue.

(At Yerrinbool a sad old man
issued from the city's gates
to meet the Traveller on the train.
I think he was the Messenger.
His tidings blew on the wind away,
Peanuts, lollies, choco . . . lay . . .)

How like the Chorus in a Play
the billboards pointed all one way
to show the God in the Machine
descending from the Empyrean,
and spoke with a united force—
Out of the Blue Comes . . . Doctor Morse!

Carried Away

'The Sailor's Girl' and 'Musket Harry',
'The Sleeping Beauty'. Scene: 'The Palace'.
Scene: 'The Wood'. How the painted branches
Enchant the heart on the pasteboard backdrop.
Cut the people out of the paper,
Paint the lady, give her emerald,
Ultramarine for the wicked uncle,
Beetling brows and black side-whiskers,
Swords and crowns and purple breeches,
Crimson lake for the canopied bed.

Put behind you the toys of childhood,
Watch expectant the empty stage,
Here's a page with a card advancing,
Act and Scene—'Bohemia's Sea-coast',
Sunburnt shepherds scything grasses.
Flourish of trumpets—enter Caesar,
Enter Anthony. 'I will tell you
The barge she sat in . . .' Imagined splendour!
Cardboard crowns and painted faces,
Playbill people, I thank you all.

My Uncle George in eighteen-eighty
Threw his wash-pan into the creek-bed,
Struck out lucky for Sullivan's Shanty,
Went on a bender and landed up
Bleary-eyed at the travelling company's
One performance—'The Miller's Daughter'.
Seeing Virtue beset, assailed,
Rose from his bench at the back of the smoke-filled
Hall, and with aim unprecedented
Shot the villain clean through the heart.

Captain Svenson

Lying in the hospital I heard the white-veiled sisters neigh,
Tossing their veils like fillies, stepping high
On the long bright shiny floors. Oh, I heard them whinny and say—

Captain Svenson will be admitted Monday,
Captain Svenson has rung to know
Does his room have a view of the harbour,
Can he listen on the radio?
The yacht-race starts on Wednesday morning—
Oh, and Sister, Sister, Sister,
The Mariners' League is on the phone,
When is the Captain's operation?
Tell them Tuesday, early in the morning.
And I thought: has he strayed from a Slessor poem?

The white-maned sisters prance like fillies
On neat white hooves from room to room
With trays, thermometers, letters, flowers,
Sharp, sharp scissors and cotton wool.
Limp as a drowned man down in the theatre
The Captain lies where he'd rather not be.
Someone listens to his ticking heart-beats:
The surgeon is snipping: one, two, three.
Back in a trice on a trolley goes the Captain,
Back to his room with a wink of the sea.

I lie on my bed and I think of the Captain
While the sisters whinny outside my door,
Their white manes tossing like the waves of the sea.
Do waves of pain wash over you, Captain,
And do you fear you are like to die?
Sister! What of Captain Svenson?

Kindly give the message that Captain Svenson
Passed a comfortable night, and is now as well—
As well, that is, as can be expected.
He holds a telescope up to the window
And rolls an eye as blue as the sea.
When I took his pulse a moment ago,
Sister, Sister how he looked at me!
Oh, Sister, Sister. Oh, Sister, Oh!

Closed Museums

Some museums speak sternly:
By caption and command
They quell and subdue.

Once, discouraged by such mandatory
Injunctions, I sat down
On the chair reserved for the attendant.

Grave blunder! Museums, I said
Have little regard
For the affection I bear them.

My companion spoke instructively:
For each museum open
Each day of the year

There are twelve, perhaps twenty,
Shut. Send, if you can
For the caretaker, the key,

It will do you no good.
Have faith, I rejoined—
Through the half-open door

Of a museum in China
We saw whitewash, step-ladders
And empty wall-space.

A devoted curator
Who stood on the threshold
Demanded our attention

While describing in detail
Ad infinitum
The objects not there.

Gwen Harwood

Out of Hell

One morning when my brain was open
I heard the neurosurgeon say
'Mental events are physical events.'
They showed me Pollock's *Lucifer*.
I felt it as a linear headache.
Skeins of enamel clogged my frontal sinus.
The aluminium paint thrilled my back fillings.
'Nothing', the surgeon said. The students
dutifully echoed, 'Nothing.'
The pretty nurse said, 'Not a trace.'

They closed my head up. Now I don't
speak, but fly at dawn and dusk
with webbing in my arms and high-
frequency shrieks. The surgeon says
'Cognitive dissonance', and asks me:
'What is it like to be a bat?'

Schrödinger's Cat Preaches to the Mice

To A. D. Hope

Silk-whispering of knife on stone,
due sacrifice, and my meat came.
Caressing whispers, then my own
choice among laps by leaping flame.

What shape is space? Space will put on
the shape of any cat. Know this:
my servant Schrödinger is gone
before me to prepare a place.

So worship me, the Chosen One
in the great thought-experiment.
As in a grave I will lie down
and wait for the Divine Event.

The lid will close. I will retire
from sight, curl up and say Amen
to geiger counter, amplifier,
and a cylinder of HCN.

When will the geiger counter feel
decay, its pulse be amplified
to a current that removes the seal
from the cylinder of cyanide?

Dead or alive? The case defies
all questions. Let the lid be locked.
Truth, from your little beady eyes,
is hidden. I will not be mocked.

Quantum mechanics has no place
for what's there without observation.
Classical physics cannot trace
spontaneous disintegration.

If the box holds a living cat
no scientist on earth can tell.
But I'll be waiting, sleek and fat.
Verily, all will not be well

if, to the peril of your souls,
you think me gone. Know that this house
is mine, that kittens by mouse-holes
wait, who have never seen a mouse.

Blackbird

In the morning my blackbird sings
  'Believe in the Trinity.'
In the evening he seems to say
  'Abandon all property.'
Song, faith and ethics from one beak—
  what a divinity!

The Flight of the Bumble Bee

Kröte plays for a fiddler scraping
  that Bee Thing from his violin.
There's little prospect of escaping
  back to the Green Room and his gin.

A piece concerned with flight—symbolic!
  he murmurs, pianissimo.
Somebody hisses 'Alcoholic'
  audibly from the nearest row.

That woman with the bust! That bumbling
  amateur with an insect heart!
Heaven preserve me from all fumbling
  spear-holders on the stage of Art.

Drunk, often. Alcoholic, never!
  Here come those octaves-and-a-third.
Madam, I could play on for ever,
  thinks Kröte, playing his absurd

pantomime of a great musician
  wrestling hard with his instrument.
The fiddler's nervous disposition
  rapidly throws him off the scent

of any flower the bee might visit—
  he scrapes beyond the normal ear.
Has Kröte drowned him out? Or is it
  a sound that only bats could hear?

The woman with the bust claps brightly,
  not sure that anything's amiss.
The fiddler bows, deciding rightly
  against an encore. Kröte's bliss

flowers in the Green Room, where restored to
  his bottle, in the grateful pause
before the storm, he can afford to
  ignore the honey of applause.

A Small Victory

Heat like a settling animal
shivers and curls across the lake.
Kröte walks from the barbecue
at which, invited by mistake,
he sat alone in silence to
the dressing shed; appears with all

eyes frankly riveted on him
in antique bathers and felt hat
and in the shallows, thus protected
from sunstroke, wades. A cheeky brat
calls in a piercing treble infected
with adult mischief, 'Can't yer swim?'

A tall man with a ginger beard
wades out, grinning, to Kröte's side
prepared to make a game of it.
Kröte waits, plump and dignified,
for him to speak. Ashore some wit
calls through loud laughter to the weird

couple, 'Christ versus Buddha! GO!'
Boredom and heat combine to breed
ill-feeling. Gingerbeard goes thrashing
wildly away at racing speed.
Kröte adjusts his hat, and, splashing
gently behind him in a slow

breast-stroke, takes no account of jeering
catcalls, but keeps his stately pace.
Gingerbeard tries some crazy clowning
quite certain that he's won the race—
kicks up his heels, pretends he's drowning,
and comes up to find Kröte peering

into his face with great concern.
They swim on. Further out from land
the water's cold. Gingerbeard swallows
too much of it; throws in his hand
and heads for shore. But Kröte follows
his lonely path; feels the sun burn

his back while water cools his chest;
swims through the temperate unfading
summers of childhood with his steady
old-fashioned stroke. Gingerbeard wading
ashore exhausted will be ready
to put his manhood to the test

but later, later. Feigning cramp
he sprawls face downward on a burning
carpet of fragile shells. They crack
sharply under Kröte's returning
footsteps. On his blistering back
Gingerbeard feels the victor's damp

chilled shell-encrusted foot repose,
as Kröte seeks the dressing shed
with muscles aching, eyeballs drumming,
heat-headache purring in his head,
remodelling his bent hat, humming
Vittoria, to put on his clothes.

Dimitris Tsaloumas

CHOGM —Melbourne 1981*

Translated by Philip Grundy

Like sulphur, like gunpowder on the surface of heaven,
bubbles have been bursting since dawn
and on the cosmic shores the angels' children
sit dangling their legs and gape at the phenomenon.
'Could it be a sun in its death-throes,
a planet in its final struggle?' But their governess,
well versed in worldly smells, upbraids them
in an angelic way. 'On the bottom of heaven,
the under-side of Earth, the bosses of the North,
swathed in furs, and the chiefs of the South,
in cut-down pants and permanently sooty,
are holding council over the woes of hunger.
And the Top Man, Old Truthful, with his white hanky,
shares at their board the flatulential fare
and seized with sharp philanthropy
pumps out messages to churn our ether.
Come in at once. Where politicians fart
is where the troubles of the angels start.'

---

* Commonwealth Heads of Government Meeting

Geoffrey Dutton

Our Crypto-Wowsers

No wowsers they, who drink and smoke
With decent wives who do not mind;
They know the latest dirty joke,
Progress never leaves them behind.
In fact, they are the ones who lead it,
Through Apex and the J.C.C.—
Public spirit for those who need it,
The ideals and smiles of Rotary,
Mateship worn on the lapel
Where every Joseph is a Joe,
And nothing is too dear to sell
And no one is too proud to know.
At night behind the sand-blasted doors
The sexes take their guided tour,
After the little woman pours
Creme de menthe and parfait amour
In stem-ware amongst soft furnishings;
A birch-tree keeps the wrought-iron cool
And a wagtail by the Holden sings
To a concrete flamingo in the pool.
The house is vacuumed every day
Which goes to prove that cleanliness,
For living the most boring way,
Is certainly next to godliness.
The good men leave no lawn untrimmed;
There is no plot but they have fenced it;
And like the wowsers they have hymned:
'There ought to be a law against it.'
Fat boys whom middle age makes lean,
They aim to keep their children chaste,
Forgetting how, by seventeen,
Their hand had slipped below the waist
And many a month was filled with fear.
Those of their contemporaries
Who have not 'settled down' are queer,
Not queer like homosexual fairies
But even worse, the queer that means
'Most peculiar', 'odd', hell-bent
Like kids on motor-bikes in jeans,

Fit for corporal punishment.
They pray their children may emerge
Not brilliant, but ordinary,
Not grow a beard, or get an urge
To study biochemistry.
They may meet New Australians, but
Never ask an Italian home;
Our broken bottles never cut,
Not like the knives they use in Rome.
Support by all means leagues and clubs
And flock to lecturers who give
Our egos little pats and rubs
And praise the way of life we live.
With luck within a hundred years
Australia will have abolished crime
And surnames, dirty books and queers,
Dry wine, old buildings, art and rhyme
(Except for commercials on TV,)
And all across the great outback,
Made safe for kiddies, there will be
A barbecue for every shack;
On greens where now the desert sprawls
Golfers will knock their little balls,
While God, in the Safety Council's Chair,
Smiles down upon Australia Fair.

Our Leisured Ladies

Tottering under a tomb of flowers,
A hat's good grief, piercing the pavement
With her heels, she empties out the hours
Wearing a slightly pained amazement.
Her children gone, her day is free,
(Her man, thank God, eats lunch away,)
And in the Mercedes, with GB,
She drives to lunch, a long display
Of speculations touched with cream,
All garnished with the shredded honour
Of those who are not what they seem,
Or worse, seem what they are. Upon her
Right, dear Mrs X, who pours
The sweet-sour sauce, alas, that Ted
Is drinking. Mrs Y abhors
The fact, but Judy's nurse is said,
Only *said*, of course, but all
You need to do is look, said now
To be taking drugs as well. The tall
New A.D.C.'s a darling, how
Perfectly he pours a gin.
He met my Annabel in Rome.
Our trip abroad was absolute heaven,
I couldn't *bear* to come back home . . .
At three they walk across the road—
An art show opened by Sir James.
After the Darlings and Dears have flowed
Someone looks at a painting. Flames
Leap from a corpse, a naked bride
Is ravished by a kangaroo.
A starving nun on a mountainside
Laughs as a crow's beak skewers her through.
My dear, I made a queer mistake,
I thought it was fruit and flowers today . . .
Back home again, she sits awake
On Sheraton. (She had to pay
A hundred guineas for each chair;
They must be genuine.) The antiques
She bought in Knightsbridge, and the pair
Of shepherdesses with rosy cheeks
Gleam that all at home is well.
She rests a little. At half past five

A visiting Englishman will tell
Her, over martinis, how alive
Australians are, full of red meat,
Unlike those decadent Europeans,
While she agrees they are effete,
And adores our lean antipodeans.
Another day will bring her bridge,
Or racing, or cocktails from the fridge,
While she, fair flower of coarser seeds
Watches the gardener dig up weeds.

Alexander Craig

The Silver Screw

Dedication: to R. A. Simpson

This is a simple fable of our time
Which you and others, Ron, may like to read,
A sort of folk-tale, told at last in rhyme.
I hope there's nothing added to impede
The story's flow, the sudden and sublime
Climax! The moral is (for all who heed):
Don't seek out devious ways to cook your goose,
And everything in nature has a use.

* * *

Once there was a young man who was born
With a silver screw inside his navel. He
Was sensitive about it, and withdrawn,
White-faced as with long worry. At his plea
To be excused from sport at Buglehorn,
The School whose boys are great by land and sea,
The Head, though first he thundered 'CAN'T YOU TAKE IT?'
Relented when he made the boy strip naked.

This was the only one who saw his shame.
(The man died not long afterwards.) Throughout
The young man's 'teens, alas, his only aim
Was how to keep the secret. To take out
A girl in summer, swimming, was the same
As being in the shower-room. No doubt
His behaviour in close dancing too could vex,
So he didn't get to know the other sex.

Morose, embittered, nervous, he would stand
Alone at parties, something like Jack Horner—
Not gleeful, though, with a plum held in his hand
But nursing his dark secret in a corner.
The young man now turned twenty. 'He's the *end*!'
Said hostesses and hosts. Without a mourner,
He passed from bright-lit evenings, lived alone
In a bachelor-flat with books and gramophone.

Soon even this was not enough. He fled
Men's haunts and sought the northern countryside.
At twenty-two he built himself a shed
Deep in a valley: gums grew far and wide,
Dark green and light; primevally the red
Rocks reared up from the hill-slopes. Unespied,
Not quite a violet by a mossy stone,
The young man hiding thought himself alone.

One day, he took a stroll along the road,
The earthen track that wound its crooked way
Beside and several miles from his abode.
Turning a corner, he saw to his dismay
A figure nearing, walking pigeon-toed:
It was a crone attempting to convey
A bundle of faggots, more than she could bear:
She stumbled and she dropped them everywhere.

His better nature triumphed. Our young man
Raced forward to assist her then, retrieved
The sticks that she'd let fall. And he began
To hoist the load upon his back. 'I grieved
To see you staggering so,' he said, 'and plan
To take these where you'd like them.' So relieved,
She piloted the hero for a mile
To a timber hut. Then turning with a smile,

She croaked: 'Young man, I'm very grateful. You
May not believe it, but I am a witch.
I'll grant you anything you ask me to:
I'll make you famous or I'll make you rich:
Speak!' First the fellow claimed his wants were few.
She seemed to look within his soul. Poor wretch,
He stammered out what he so long had brooded
And told her how the silver screw intruded.

'Go up that hill,' she pointed to the right,
'And half-way to its summit you will find
A flat grey rock—not red. Go up to-night.
At twelve sit naked on that stone. And mind,
You must be there exactly then; for right
Upon the stroke of midnight, 'tis designed
Your wish be granted unto you!' (*You* may
Think *this* old-fashioned: witches talk that way.)

The young man did as he was told. Alone,
He climbed the hill at half-past ten and sat
Upon the rock, the squat grey ledge of stone.
He practised sitting this way and then that,
And squirmed and shivered there until the moon
Had mounted to its highest sphere. Then at
The stroke of midnight, all about the hill,
The heavens were dark and tense, the air was still,

When suddenly, from that black and glimmering sky,
A shaft of light descended. Down it sped
A ghostly screw-driver—swift to apply
Itself to turn the navel screw! The thread
Gleamed and revolved for hours, but finally
Its glittering silver length hung overhead
Then dwindled in the darkness. Now the column
Of light sheered off. The moon beamed, round and solemn.

'At last,' the young man cried, 'at last I'm free!'
He looked, and sure enough the screw *was* gone:
'No more my dreadful shame can trouble me!'
Now on his waving arms the moonlight shone
And on his face, transfigured in its glee:
'My life will be so happy from now on!
No more I'll be afraid that girls may scoff!'
He leapt up to his feet. And his bum fell off.

Dennis Davison

To Her Coy Lover

My party dress and talk were aimed at you;
I wanted it, I ached all bloody night;
It's hell to think that bitch enjoys the rite
Of love (is that the phrase the prudish coo?)
When my hot body needs your body too.
You squeezed my tits and hugged my belly tight,
With drunken courage when I dimmed the light;
Why can't we go to bed like you two do?
The music stops and, bastard, so do you,
Scuttling to sweetie in your sickening fright:
You're bold enough when dancing cheek to cheek,
So long as wifie's not around to squeak.

Mrs Homer T. Mickiewicz

I believe in the American Way of Life
But not the American lay of wife
(Somebody else's), though I encourage
My husband to screw his boss's
If it will get him an executive's office
With an ivory phone and a wall-to-wall
Ulcer. I'm in debt up to the tits,
The kids are out of control, Homer
Sees the headshrinker once a week,
Color T.V. threatens our sex-life,
I dream about niggers burning
Our beautiful uptown residence
(Unpaid for) and standing for the Senate.
One of the girls smokes pot, the boy
Is a college bum, my priest brother
Has just married an ex-nun, I admit
I take the Pill, it's okay for the Pope
To talk holy but he doesn't have to
Sell panties in a local store
Afternoons, like I do, to pay
The freezer and the electric barbecue.
Sure, I'm an easy target for the liberals,
I support film censorship, am unsure
About war, vote Democrat sometimes,
Love my husband most times, drink
Too much gin at parties, hate pornography,
Hate high society richbitches,
Spoil my children, never read science fiction,
Lead a blameless moral life,
Am a half-educated, middle-aged,
White, poor middle-class, Irish-Polish
American. This is a cry for help.

Nancy Keesing

Procedures

I seem to have got myself onto the end of this list.
Please initial and pass on.
Five other people have read it and left their initials
which do so little resemble their actual names,
as their names so little resemble their actual faces,
and their faces so often belie their words and deeds,
and their words and deeds are not their intimate selves.
How did they look when they read this wretched memo?
Did they frown at their OUT tray as I do now at mine?
Was one of them tempted, as I, to impress a kiss
in greasy lipstick instead of inked initials?
I pick up my biro. So what!
        And, anyway,
                who is
                    N.K.?

Reflections on a Guest Speaker

Scrubbed clean: steps, hall, chairs, girls—but mocked
by chalky air that will not settle
the school assembles. Mums arrive.
A stray dog slinks. Reward of mettle,

pile upon pile of shining books
wink at the carols, distract the speeches
of: always-this-important-year
and, always-times-we-live-in teaches

something or other. Always peril,
youth much wilder, never older—
T.V., pop songs, parties, hair-bleach . . .
Hidden just behind the shoulder

of each dying year, and never quite spoken
lurk babies—source of all the bother,
unconceived (we hope), unborn,
rioting in their wailing smother

of washing, brick veneer, prams, lollies,
dolls and Kinder, Primary, High.
I have suffered thirty Speech Days
child, parent, speaker . . . my, oh my!

Isobel Robin

The Invitreous Advent of Septimus
or
Don't Freeze Your Assets in the Sperm Bank, Dad

There was panic in the Common Room, commotion in the Lab.,
And the Chief Researcher poured himself a drink,
For his blonde research assistant, while escaping from his grab,
Had slipped, and spilled the ova down the sink.

There was consternation, conference, an instant seminar,
And the Junior on the team was seen to squirm
For just one second earlier he'd emptied out a jar
Of superfluous, thawed-out, unwanted sperm.

Summon the technicians! Call a plumber! Call a nurse!
God knows what's down there—heaven knows what brews!
With wrench and spanner rampant, with a grunt and with a curse,
They sought for sperm and ova in the ooze.

Now one brave spermatozoön, sensing destiny or fate
And heading where his instinct seemed to point,
Went zooming through the plumbing till he found his ovoid mate
And merged with her down in the elbow joint.

With cheers and with Eurekas it was filtered from the sludge,
It was cared for, it was cosseted and prized.
For the Chief Researcher knew for sure that no one would begrudge
Its right to life now it was fertilised.

But who would be its mother? Who would nurture and gestate?
What warm, responding uterus would bear?
The blonde research assistant said 'I'll be its surrogate.
Well, after all, it's my fault that it's there.'

Up spoke the anxious Junior. 'Marry me! I'll be its Dad.
I never shirked a duty in my life!'
So the ovum found its sanctum, and a bouncing little lad
Was delivered nine months later to the wife.

They called the baby Septimus. He flourished and won prizes
At baby shows, and later on at school.
He won ribbons for athletics, he won cups of different sizes,
He made the top *Cum Laude*, keen and cool.

A Professor of Genetics he became—the youngest ever—
A few years after he had won the Rhodes.
But if scandal strikes, it's useless to be wonderfully clever
When excusing aberrative episodes.

And scandal struck at Septimus. His sinkular conception
Had burned into his psychic counterpoint.
In spite of icy showers, embarrassment, deception,
He fixated on a nifty elbow joint.

At governors' receptions, at parties and at balls,
If they knew beforehand Septimus was coming,
The word would go before him, echo grimly down the halls:
'He'll *be* here. Hurry—Lock away the plumbing.'

They'd find him in the laundry, they'd find him in the loo,
Tail over tip examining the pipes.
He would steal a plastic bucket, pinch a monkey wrench, unscrew,
And search for siblings—his own prototypes.

It meant the end for Septimus. It ruined his career.
He tried to find work as a plumber's mate
But only found the dole queue. He declined, and now I fear
He's unscrewing joints inside the Pearly Gate.

So I beg, with the restraint of an exploding super-nova,
Go on tiptoes, hold your breath, and—damn you—THINK!
Be careful when you're handling somebody else's ova
Or tipping heaven-knows-what down the sink.

Frogs' Eggs

Uniformed for a Ladies' College—
Nine-year-olds, bemused by knowledge
When all that we really craved to know
Was 'where did I come from? Where do I go?
What makes babies? And how? And why?'
And 'Thora Dawkin has swallowed a fly.
Is she going to die?'

Miss McRory, maiden lady,
Stout, black brogues and an eerie, shady
Green straw hat on her flame-hot bun,
Pursed her face against the sun,
Flexed her corset to ease exertion
And marched us on a nature excursion.

Later, at the tadpole creek
She let us paddle, gather, seek
In cool, wet eddies on cool, pale stones,
Slime in our toes and joy in our bones
And a century sun that withered the sky.
While Thora, who had swallowed a fly,
Could sicken and die.

Tadpoles flicked between our legs,
Squirmy, spermy, fruit of eggs;
In still, dark pools near mossy logs
Lay spotted jelly, promised frogs.
Vestigial truths from mysterious places
Stirred, untaught, across our faces.

Bulge-eyed frogs with catapult legs—
Amniotic sud of eggs
Already shaping tadpole tails—
Wine of Life in our jam-jar grails.
What made it start? And how? And why?
But Thora Dawkin, unwilling to die,
Disgorged her fly.

The long march back—a furnace mile
In giggling, straggling crocodile;
Miss McRory, forty, queasy,
Wondering why she felt uneasy
On currents of innocent, pristine glee,
That summer of nineteen-thirty-three.

Puritan school-ma'am, rest in peace
For answers come when the questions cease.
Those summer-wondering, pre-pubescent
Waders in waters of evanescent
Ignorance, learned how and why;
And time has fed us on many a fly
But we didn't all die.

Vincent Buckley

Teaching German Literature

I teach German literature, and this is how it goes:
Schiller, Boll and Holderlin, and everybody knows
that Bertolt turned on Thomas Mann and punched him on the nose,
and Goethe married Clara Kronk and Clara married Wagner.

Hardy is a proximist and Philip Larkin hates
walking past the neighbours' children hanging on the gates.
Keats was orphaned, Donne was bent, and Shelley went out
drowning,
and Wordsworth married Sara Dronk and Sara married Browning.

T. S. Eliot, marvellous boy, grew up with a mitre;
even in dark Russell Square you wouldn't find much brighter,
Furster Rilke knew a duchess, Trudi von Bachbeiter,
and Mara married Pablo Yeats and Pablo never married.

The greats of German literature are in the dressing room,
Lotte Lenya, Suky Tawdry, fending off life's gloom,
Hans Otto Eller Manzenberger smiling at his poem,
and Clara married Leslie Liszt and Leslie married Magna.

And Goethe married Clara Kronk and Clara married Wagner.

Grace Perry

Canberra City Sunday

Plastic mouldings from breakfast cereal boxes,
empty roads are toy circles and squares,
houses and highrise multicoloured blocks
a child might stack and topple in despair.

Regimented motels welcome lovers.
Arch and fountain project the double need.
The parched metropolis protects herself;
moat and tower defend the gesture and the deed.

Time returns to ancient aqueous origins.
Men and women scream and hide their heads
hearing the borborygmi of the brontosaurus
above the gurgling of the waterbeds.

R. F. Brissenden

Zoology AO1

(iii)

Hickman, Hickman and Hickman: 'Integrated Principles of Zoology'
Birds are indeed highly social creatures

This is a photograph of 'Martha'
Who died in 1914.
She was the last of the Passenger Pigeons,
Ectopistae migratorii
That once darkened the skies of North America.
In 1869
Hunters shot seven point five
Million
Passenger Pigeons from a single nesting site.

When he was a boy,
The senior author of this text
Cleveland P. Hickman
Saw 'Martha'
Some years before she died
In the Cincinnati Zoo.

The Canberra Blues

Let's sing a song of Canberra, the nation's capital:
It's a very pretty city, but it's got no heart at all.
  You get those bad Canberra blues,
  Get on the booze;
  You get those awful Canberra blues.

We drink a lot of beer here, we've got a lot of friends;
It's like being at a party, but the party never ends.
  You get those bad Canberra blues,
  Stay on the booze;
  You get those awful Canberra blues.

I came to this fair city, looking round for work.
That was twenty years ago today—I'm still a base-grade clerk.
  I've got those bad Canberra blues
  Which I can't lose;
  I've got those bad bureaucratic blues.

Got no little girlie to cheer up my life—
If ever I get any loving, it's with somebody else's wife.
  I've got those bad Canberra blues.
  I'm on the loose.
  I've got those mean adulterous blues.

Go east or west in this fair city, of one thing you may be sure:
You'll see the same damned faces that you saw the day before.
  You'll get those bad Canberra blues,
  Get on the booze;
  You'll get those dreadful capital city blues.

You're broke and you go into a bar, no matter when or where—
The mates that you've bought drinks for will be somewhere else, not there.
  You'll have those bad Canberra blues
  Without the booze;
  You'll have those awful dry old blues.

Some people say they'll never stay, it's driving them insane:
They get right out of Canberra by the quickest train or plane.
  They leave those bad Canberra blues,
  They leave the booze;
  They leave those awful Canberra blues.

But here's a little mystery I'd like you to explain:
Those folks who run away from here, they all come back again—
Back to those bad Canberra blues,
Back to the booze,
Back to those governmental, bureaucratic,
University, academic,
Matrimonial, very adulterous,
Always alcoholic blues.

The Back-Blocks Academic

I'm a back-blocks academic, which may give rise to mirth,
But selection committees know me well from Brisbane through to Perth;
I've often been short-listed for many a famous chair
But somehow or other, I don't know why, I've never quite got there.

Hoorah, my application's in
I've got three referees;
The field is strictly limited,
There's no one from overseas;
I'm wearing my suit to seminars,
I've burnt my party card;
And if I'm overlooked again,
Then times is bloody hard.

I don't write letters to the press, but articles instead;
I've tried out every possible lurk for a man to get ahead.
The songs I sing at parties are less bawdy than before;
I've even drunk the VC's scotch—a man cannot do more.

Hoorah, my application's in
I've got three referees;
The field is strictly limited,
There's no one from overseas;
I'm wearing my suit to seminars,
I've burnt my party card;
And if I'm overlooked again,
Then times is bloody hard.

With a Glass of Spaetlaese

To A. D. Hope

'Never trust a water-drinker,'
  The wise old Roman said,
'To put a pen to paper
  Or take the muse to bed.

'For songs and epic verses
  Of the true heroic shape
Are only made by poets
  Who love the sun-blessed grape;

'And those nine lively ladies
  In Apollo's chorus line
Keep all their charms for lovers
  Whose kisses taste of wine.'

Two thousand years of drinking—
  Two thousand years of song—
Have gone to show that Horace
  Was much more right than wrong.

The wandering scholar-poet
  Wrote his verses at an inn
And the bad boys from Black Mountain
  All mixed vermouth with their gin.

Ben Jonson loved canary;
  Claret made John Keats sing;
For Byron hock and soda-
  water was the thing.

Shakespeare drank his sherries
  Beneath his mulberry trees;
And even old Tom Eliot
  Sipped a little port with cheese.

But it takes a mighty drinker
  To make a noble song:
So raise your glass to Alec—
  Long may he live; and long

Late-pick a poem each morning;
  Talk with his friends at night;
And drink each day his bottle
  Of cheerful red or white!

Peter Porter

A Consumer's Report

The name of the product I tested is *Life*,
I have completed the form you sent me
and understand that my answers are confidential.

I had it as a gift,
I didn't feel much while using it,
in fact I think I'd have liked to be more excited.
It seemed gentle on the hands
but left an embarrassing deposit behind.
It was not economical
and I have used much more than I thought
(I suppose I have about half left
but it's difficult to tell)—
although the instructions are fairly large
there are so many of them
I don't know which to follow, especially
as they seem to contradict each other.
I'm not sure such a thing
should be put in the way of children—
It's difficult to think of a purpose
for it. One of my friends says
it's just to keep its maker in a job.
Also the price is much too high.
Things are piling up so fast,
after all, the world got by
for a thousand million years
without this, do we need it now?
(Incidentally, please ask your man
to stop calling me 'the respondent',
I don't like the sound of it.)
There seems to be a lot of different labels,
sizes and colours should be uniform,
the shape is awkward, it's waterproof
but not heat resistant, it doesn't keep
yet it's very difficult to get rid of:
whenever they make it cheaper they seem
to put less in—if you say you don't
want it, then it's delivered anyway.
I'd agree it's a popular product,
it's got into the language; people

even say they're on the side of it.
Personally I think it's overdone,
a small thing people are ready
to behave badly about. I think
we should take it for granted. If its
experts are called philosophers or market
researchers or historians, we shouldn't
care. We are the consumers and the last
law makers. So finally, I'd buy it.
But the question of a 'best buy'
I'd like to leave until I get
the competitive product you said you'd send.

A Bag of Pressmints

In the middle of a difficult book,
called I see 'The Allegy of Love',
I ask through a cloud of interference
or is it the Claud of Unknowing
why the spectral voice of truth
is fiddling with my chosen words.

It's not that these are simple messages,
God getting in touch with Pharaoh
or the Dog of Death mooching with the Furies,
rather it's the sky unscrambling
in its joy of chaos: everything in place
but huge disorder in our view of it.
The world was misprinted its first day.
In the beginning was the lord;
Coercion or Correction was His name;
He hungered in the Book of Genocide
and the great beast, the Adversary,
was Grauniad, the ever-eating mother,
appearing soon afterwards at the breakfast table
as reason's voice, The Guardian.

This is to snatch significance
from decadence of purpose. Language,
though it says it knows its place,
will always try to be subversive,
telling the eight a.m. analysand
that jokes or tumblersfull of sherry
won't blunten Grandma's teeth one bit
and little girls will never get out of the wood
even if they do know how to spell.

Here it comes again, like an ellipse
of the sun. I'm correcting proofs
in a dream and find I've written
'Patriots always stand for the
National Anathema.' And two lines later,
'Seven Hypes of Ambiguity'—
I'm quite relieved my misprints
make such sense. A pity my books
are kept so plain by too much meaning.

Help yourself to a strong mint from my bag,
it will take responsibility off your breath.

Bruce Dawe

Weather Forecast

I've just been told by One Who Knows
  That things are again under way,
That the sails now tease with a genial breeze
  And the rigging's beginning to sway,
That the storms are past, every hurricane blast
  Blown clear out of breath in the bay,
That any time now, on the topmost bough,
  Noah's raven will burst into song—
In my innocent youth I'd have taken this for truth
  And I'd pass the good word along
In another bar, to some other galah,
  For nothing, gratis, free,
Had I not overheard this same wise bird
  Who told ME good and strong
Tell the bloke over there with a similar air
  Of confidence as he told me—
That the skies were lowering, the problems towering
  The best years certainly behind
That the winds were up and the seas getting rough
  And the ship was steering blind,
There were reefs ahead and the captain dead
  And the less said the better for the crew,
But that, bound to the mast, we might just outlast
  The worst that the storm could do!

Genesis

School began again this week . . .

Mincing in their brand-new tunics,
Cocky in their blue and grey,
Shouldering their cardboard school-bags,
Getting in each other's way,
Entering their different class-rooms
(Like old 'lags' to whom all's one!),
Stabbing first flies with new biros,
Watching, corner-eyed, the sun
No longer at their beck and calling
Answering, like them, the bell,
Carefully printing names on note-books
In a script too soon pell-mell,
Opening with sinking spirits
Text-books whose right answers loom
Like jet 'planes so far above them,
Waiting for the sonic boom
Of comprehension, eating lunches,
Or part thereof: tooth-rotting cakes,
Mind-destroying Fizzi-Cola,
Dumping wholesome snacks Mum makes
In the school incinerator—
Ah, what ink-stained webs we weave
When first from Eden's garden sending
Little Adam, little Eve!

Under a Cloud

A black cloud lies over Millmerran,
  Eastward the eye can see
Not a solitary sign of existence—
  O bring back Toowoomba to me!

A stranger came by here last Tuesday,
  A fear-driven look in his eye.
When I asked him from what he was fleeing,
  'I flee, sir,' he said, 'from the fly!'

'I've fought the Wandoan mosquito,
  Knee-deep in dead corpses I've stood,
Mt Lamington leeches have left me
  Down to my last pint of blood.

'I've been stung by the Mungallala bull-ant
  More times than I care to repeat,
The Great Northern Tree-Crab has nipped me
  And practically severed both feet.

'But these, I aver, are mere child's-play
  Compared to the flies you may meet
In the wilds of the new Civic Centre,
  The back-blocks of Margaret Street.

'At some city hotels I've seen them
  On pay-day in great droves appear,
And stand there ten-deep on the bar-top
  To beat a slow man to his beer!

'But what really makes a man ropeable,
  What makes a man really upset
Is the way they say 'Cheers!' to each other
  Before quenching their thirst in your sweat!'

Lights! Lights!

Well, they're good studs if only half of what
They say is true, their roving camera's eye
Catching them (with heady frequency)
In the act of slinging a leg across some thigh
Or other, while the stars (those chaste pimps) wait
For stage directions . . .
Some continually languish,
Satiated lovers, others distinguish
Themselves by rapt dissection of their anguish.

And all cry from the housetops of their verse
Their right to call balls balls, etc., hauling
These hairy mysteries forth to be adored . . .
Ah, why should fierce strict virgins rave and curse
Because such fine young buckos by their calling
Now prove the penis mightier than the sword?

On the Conferring of an Honorary Doctorate of Law on a Politician

Let snakes be shod! Prepare the mare her nest!
Let every fabulous unlikely thing
Come true to match this curious happening!
See where he trots in academic gown
His second honorary doctorate on
—Was ever man so naked though well-dressed?

Philip Martin

Bequest

To those who never read, I leave my writings,
Just what they never wanted, tunes for the deaf,
Skywriting for the blind. To plagiarists,
A style, if not the taste for it. To critics,
Pushing aside their flagons to despatch
The work of half a life in half an hour,
This Christian hope: May they not wake in Limbo
Blushing. To the politicians of my birthplace
Who, not being God, do not provide: in time
Of drought, a cup of muddy water. And
To my coolest mistress, my electric blanket.

Thanks for the Stockings

My poems, Nancy, seldom rhyme, but this one
Should, maybe? At our one meeting, I
Spoke of the woman in my life, the patterned
Stockings I'd tried to find her. You asked 'How
Tall is she?' Now you send me a slim
Parcel: a pair of patterned stockings, and
The right size too! How often in the whole
History of the race has any woman
Given a man a pair of stockings for
Another, a woman whom she hasn't even
Met? . . . And still no rhymes. Instead the sense
Runs on (and on), and rightly, since she's yet
To see your stockings: hers. And when she makes them
Hers, at length, then's the best time for rhyme.

Philip Grundy

Hymn to Canberra Queen of the Plains and Hills

(A National Anthem for the A.C.T.)

When God beneath the Southern Cross
   Created land and sea
The choicest spot His Finger touched
   Was called the A.C.T.
Our hills bedecked with Eucalypts,
   Our Lake is girt by Land;
Within our City's noble streets
   Imposing Buildings stand.
Here mighty Statesmen labour for
   Our Country's common weal,
And Public Servants work to show
   The Loyalty they feel.

Chorus

Brisbane and Sydney and Melbourne and Perth
Hobart and Adelaide, what are they worth?
Villages, all of them, greet them with mirth!
We'll fight for Canberra, Land of our birth.

In glorious Homes our people dwell,
   Both humble and aloof,
Their sturdy Walls of brick veneer,
   Of solid Tiles their roof.
Each Suburb here with quiet pride
   Our Heroes' fame proclaims,
While bosky streets preserve for aye
   The mem'ry of their Names.
For where God's handiwork reveals
   The Beauty of His Plan,
The N.C.D.C.* daily adds
   The handiwork of Man.

---

* The National Capital Development Commission

Who would our Land's armorial pride
  In Tidbinbilla view
May there the stalwart Emu see,
  The sturdy Kangaroo;
While midst the Melaleuca of
  Our native Habitat
One may behold the Possum and
  The lissom Feral Cat.
Nor lacks our Lake the finny tribe
  That swims there without fuss,
And in our Streams float Monotremes,
  The loyal Platypus.

O Canberra! O Canberra! where
  Mighty Mountains roll,
Our Planners made thee beautiful,
  Our City with a Soul.
Yea, Canberra, thy People are
  A great and happy Band
Of Citizens rejoicing that
  Thou hast been fully planned!
Let lesser breeds within the States
  In envy scoff and sneer:
We know that if they had the Chance
  They would be living here!

A Democratic Benefaction

For A. D. Hope, the Master of light verse

Lord Avebury, although a peer,
Had views which Bishops of the House
Considered odd, perverse and queer.
A Buddhist he: to every louse

And nit he bowed in Eastern fashion
And held for larger beasts a love
Nigh tantamount to human passion.
From death he sought no Life Above

But rather a Reincarnation
As dog or cat or other pet
So venerated by his nation.
And so, when death approached he let

His lack of faith in Resurrection
Lead him to will his working bits
To pre-med students for dissection,
Or else as Health Care benefits

(For where an organ here and there
Had not become too worn and shoddy,
Doctors might use it as a spare
To transplant to some other body.)

So far so good, but what of those
Remaining pieces of his frame,
His arms and legs, his ears and nose,
Should he consign them to the flame

Or bury them in sodden earth,
Disposing of his fleshly trash
So that the cycle of Rebirth
Would bring them back as worm . . . or ash?

Such thoughts appalled him: he abhorred,
With Buddhist faith and British taste,
The notion that a noble Lord
Should be dissolved and go to waste.

He therefore gave as his bequest
His meaty bones to make high tea
(Or lunch perhaps) for every guest
In London's Dogs' Home, Battersea.

The mutts and bitzers in the pound
  Barked in delirium at the news,
For while a true-bred basset hound
  Might royally dine in London mews

Or Mayfair flats on caviar
  Or Kobe steak massaged with beer,
How privileged those mongrels are
  Whose jaws may chomp a British Peer!

Alas, their rapture swiftly died;
  Their gaolers, wowsers to a man,
Announced that they were horrified:
  'Dog food is packaged in a can

Or hard, dry biscuits; Dine and Pal
  Are suited to the canine tooth.
Blue blood's not for the animal
  And chomping earls we deem uncouth.'

Our hero, thwarted in his wish
  To feed the doggies, changed his notion,
Switched his affections to the fish,
  Consigned his body to the ocean.

Now English lads who're indigent
  Yet anxious to impress their Dinah
Without financial detriment,
  May bless the name of that consignor:

For common folk, though base and low,
  So be they dine on fish and chips,
Through Avebury's benefaction know
  Nobility has brushed their lips;

And though the portion may be small
  It graces every humble board,
While no man lacks the wherewithal
  To feast upon a British Lord.

Keith Harrison

Picasso's Bull

Irreverent replies to
'The Creativity Question'

1

You see, Picasso was in love with bulls.
He kept one in the basement of his home
And some have claimed he fed it daffodils
And bits of shrimp he snaffled from the Dome.
Be that as it may be, he always had
Bull on his mind. But it was Gertrude Stein
Who touched it off—'Time to get going, Dad.
We need a Biggie: Five by Twenty-nine.'

Now Gertrude knew that Pablo couldn't draw
So she and Alice helped. 'Something un-dull,
Let's call it *Guernica.*' 'O.K. that sure
Has poetry.' He started on the bull
But never got it right. Said Saint Gertrude:
'We'll sell it off, but crude is crude.'

2

Then there was Ezra and that Chinese story:
When widow Fenellosa came to town
With a stash of notes and hunted Ezra down,
'Please English these' she said—'Professor Mori
And Ernest worked a decade at this task.'
Ezra who didn't know from crud one word
In all the notes, pounced like a hungry bird.
There are some things a poet doesn't ask.

And soon all London had discovered China,
That is to say, twelve people at the least.
The critics beamed: 'There has been nothing finer
From Mr Pound. Rare essence of the East;
Even when wrong, he's right—what more to say?'
He even conned the Chinese in Cathay.

3

Basho was such another. You know that book
The Journal of the Long Trip to the North?
He never wrote it. There was a winsome cook

Who kept Basho from ever 'venturing forth'.
A gorgeous girl who rubbed his back—and more:
For sometimes she would murmur in her sleep
These perfect haiku—gave him fifty-four!
He stole them, father, and without a beep.

That's why he sent disciples scurrying off
Every which way to keep meticulous notes.
He wanted them out, he couldn't get enough
Of the toothsome cook. He took their anecdotes
Called them his own, and the cook's haiku too.
Way to go, Basho baby—bully for you!

4

'I've got a problem and it goes like this:
That cod-head Burbage calls for another one
That lets his boy-friend dress up like a miss
And mince about the stage like a simpleton.
Burbage I owe five pounds. But Cavendish
Has paid me for the next three things I do;
Cavandish's daughter's a little dish
And Cavendish loves my brother. This is a stew.

I'll give them bits and pieces. Something
About an ass (be careful), a fairy queen;
Something recherche on a lecherous king:
A wet-dream fantasy WHAT MIGHT HAVE BEEN.
Jesus, two plays by Thursday. What a fix!'

[Bill Shakespeare, from a journal, '96]

5

Some lie, some sweat for weeks—that clever men
Can hone their teeth and try to chew their brains
For anecdotes, or hints, or dreams, and then
Devise some theory that at last 'explains'.
'Neurotics', 'rebels', 'creative will' and 'drive':
Less difficult, more difficult than that.
From all their scribblings what can we derive?
A ten-year answer makes ten scholars fat.

A captive fly sings in the sticky strings;
An elephant may tup a cockatoo
And lizards piddle when they wash their wings.
Study their ways and learn what artists do!
Ah, let's give up this mental push and pull
And say of Pablo that he loved his bull.

Chris Wallace-Crabbe

Exit the Players

It is over. Self-mortifying Hamlet
gets up and puts his sword back on the shelf;
Laertes, unbloody, shuts his manila folder;

the Queen, who moved two separate amendments,
thinks Yorick played the fool offensively;
Horatio had the numbers this afternoon

and buffaloed through a policy decision
the Ghost would not have stomached;
Denmark is feeling just a wee bit whacked.

Ophelia's hair is dry: she didn't say much
but wouldn't mind slipping over to the pub
with Rosencrantz—why does he have to keep nattering

to the King? It's drinking time. Stiff Guildenstern
will not forgive Polonius and, to boot,
has lost his biro somewhere round the place.

It could have been worse. The dead all kept their tempers,
Gertrude cracked several, Hamlet one good joke
and they got through the whole agenda, perhaps because

Fortinbras is still on sabbatical leave.

Citizen

The roofs of cars were crusted thick with frost
And ice was notable on every pool;
Blue children stalked in overcoats and gloves
Past the Immaculate Heart of Mary School.

And where he walked the traffic ran one way—
Toward the sacred ritual of work—
While hasty breakfasts rumbled in those cars
Whose flying mud had stopped him with a jerk.

On villa, cottage, sweet-shop, bungalow,
Schoolroom and Gentlemen's, the morning grinned
Facetiously. He quietly picked his way
Among the houses where the world had sinned.

Now schizoid barbers packed their shaving gear,
Uncomfortable lovers caught the train
And everyone rushed. It was at times like this
That decent violence beset his brain.

'Complacent city with your brazen bells
And morning song . . .' He called for words to cease
For citizens to know their proper hells
And anger to bloom green upon the trees.

The Collective Invention

Wanting a myth for blowing up the gods
In his flowing silver cape and plastic wings
Captain Melbourne zooms over Lonsdale Street.

His faithful girl assistants screech below
In their custom runabout:
Their T-shirts bear the sweet inscription JUSTICE
And they wear it well.

Admiringly, the crims and their dwarf henchmen
Hustle away,
Skulk underneath the overpasses,
Terrified of the sterling Captain
And those just bosoms busy on their trail.

Glancing up from our sandwiches, if we're lucky
We might spot him gliding overhead
In his line of business,
Doing the common good all day long,
A handful of thunderbolts in his shoulder holster.

O Captain Melbourne, man of the wind and rain,
You are our hero,
Save us from northern weakness,
Continue still to zap and biff and pow.

Whisky

We call it lively water for its burn of breath
Keeps winter awhile away
Even the sprinting halfhearted Australian winters
Which fade and bloom the same day.

It is Ossian's ichor, Jameson's god on wheels;
Can transform five o'clock
From the depths of the bullshit soul by leaping
Straight to the brain or cock.

We need not celebrate it with a champagne toast:
Two fingers of gold will do.
It swims around in the back of my eyes transforming
Every linoleum view.

It stains our veins telling today tomorrow
Has better things to do.

I'm yabbering away nineteen to the dozen,
Some of which may be true.

Clive James

The Book of My Enemy Has Been Remaindered

The book of my enemy has been remaindered
And I am pleased.
In vast quantities it has been remaindered.
Like a van-load of counterfeit that has been seized
And sits in piles in a police warehouse,
My enemy's much-prized effort sits in piles
In the kind of bookshop where remaindering occurs.
Great, square stacks of rejected books and, between them, aisles
One passes down reflecting on life's vanities,
Pausing to remember all those thoughtful reviews
Lavished to no avail upon one's enemy's book—
For behold, here is that book
Among these ranks and banks of duds,
These ponderous and seemingly irreducible cairns
Of complete stiffs.

The book of my enemy has been remaindered
And I rejoice.
It has gone with bowed head like a defeated legion
Beneath the yoke.
What avail him now his awards and prizes,
The praise expended upon his meticulous technique,
His individual new voice?
Knocked into the middle of next week
His brainchild now consorts with the bad buys,
The sinkers, clinkers, dogs and dregs,
The Edsels of the world of movable type,
The bummers that no amount of hype could shift,
The unbudgeable turkeys.

Yea, his slim volume with its understated wrapper
Bathes in the glare of the brightly jacketed *Hitler's War Machine*,
His unmistakably individual new voice
Shares the same scrapyard with a forlorn skyscraper
Of *The Kung-Fu Cookbook*,
His honesty, proclaimed by himself and believed in by others,
His renowned abhorrence of all posturing and pretence,
Is there with *Pertwee's Promenades and Pierrots—*
One Hundred Years of Seaside Entertainment,
And (oh, this above all) his sensibility,

His sensibility and its hair-like filaments,
His delicate, quivering sensibility is now as one
With *Barbara Windsor's Book of Boobs*,
A volume graced by the descriptive rubric
'My boobs will give everyone hours of fun.'

Soon now a book of mine could be remaindered also,
Though not to the monumental extent
In which the chastisement of remaindering has been meted out
To the book of my enemy,
Since in the case of my own book it will be due
To a miscalculated print run, a marketing error—
Nothing to do with merit.
But just supposing that such an event should hold
Some slight element of sadness, it will be offset
By the memory of this sweet moment.
Chill the champagne and polish the crystal goblets!
The book of my enemy has been remaindered
And I am glad.

Will Those Responsible Come Forward?

May the Lord have mercy on all those peoples
Who suffer from a perversion of religion—
Or, to put it in a less equivocating way,
Who suffer from an excess of religion—
Or, to come right out with it,
Who suffer from religion.

Let him tell those catholic protestants or protestant catholics
Who in Northern Ireland go to bed on Saturday night
Looking forward to a morning of Holy Worship
That just this once they should make other plans—
Have a heavy cold, a stomach upset or a pulled hamstring
Severe enough to render them immobile,
With something similar for their children—
So that they will not be there to form a congregation
In a church just big enough for a small massacre.
Arrange this reprieve, Lord,
And if you can't manage that much then for Christ's sake
Hand the whole deal over to Allah.

May the Lord with the assistance of Allah
Give heed to the cries of those children in Beirut
Who have the dubious luck to be ten years old and under
While dwelling in the vicinity of a PLO faction
Currently being wiped out by another PLO faction,
And kindly swing it so that the incoming rockets
Do not dismember their small persons irreparably.
Children older than ten years we will give up on,
Not wanting the moon,
And their mothers, needless to say, are for the high jump.
Fix it, Lord. Get Al on to it,
And if it turns out to be more than you can handle
Raise Jehovah on the horn.

May the Lord and Allah with Jehovah's proverbial
In-depth back-up and sales apparatus
Make a concerted effort to cut the crap,
For the following reasons among others:

Lest at least two kinds of Christians during their annual shoot-out
Bisect an old lady who hears the word 'Duck!'
But can't hit the deck because of sciatica
(May her stoop be steep)—

Lest the Druze and the Jews or the Juze and the Drews,
When shelling each other from somewhere each side
Of a ridge or a bridge,
Cascade hot shrapnel on the intervening hospital
Whose patients suffer from mental disorders,
And thus exacerbate in those unstable minds
An already acute sense of insecurity
(May their strait-jackets be flak-jackets)—

Lest Iraq and Iran or Iran and Iraq go to rack and ruin
Not just in the standard Islamic manner
Of finding each other insufficiently fanatical,
But with an ironic new wrinkle
By which the hitherto unapproachably sordid
Ayatollah or Arsola
Is upstaged by his own appointee,
That even more sadistic fuckwit and fruitcake
The Hayula or Payola,
Who has women tortured in front of their husbands
As a forceful reminder, no doubt supererogatory,
That you can't fight central mosque
(May their screams be deafening)—

Who also, if that doesn't do the trick,
Has the children tortured along with their mothers
(May they all go crazy quickly),
The object being to make the fathers admit
That they plotted the regime's overthrow—
A pretty fantastic charge when you consider
That the regime's overthrow hasn't yet been accomplished
By Allah functioning either on his tod
Or in combination with the Lord, Jehovah,
Buddha, the Great Spirit and each and every other
Recognised form of God—

Always supposing that They are working on it.
Always supposing that They care
About that or anything else.

But this is the sin of despair.

Geoff Page

A Toper Speaks

Wrest me, Lord, from the grip of Bacchus;
I shall not be a sot.
Let me be called no nobbler
Nor any vile tosspot.

I will not be a frothblower,
Get sozzled, soused or soaked;
I will not guzzle, swig or swill,
Tipple, quaff or tope.

I'll tread the path of rectitude,
Imbibe no vinous brews;
My nose will be no grog blossom
Nor redden in the stews.

I shall not touch strong waters,
No one shall say I sinned.
Let no one call me boiled or pickled
Or three sheets to the wind.

Tonight I'll touch no malt, no rye,
No eau de vie nor gin;
No bourbon will I touch, nor scotch,
Nor what's called mother's ruin.

God save me from the jim-jams,
The heebie-jeebies, too.
I'll be no foul inebriate
Astonished by the dew.

I'll climb up on the wagon
and (veering straight ahead)
The Women's Christian Temperance League
Will see me into bed.

They'll nuzzle me all night with words,
The ones we used to use,
Direct from Roget 949,
Almost as nice as booze.

Giving It Up

'Young man,' (the voice is almost kind)
'It seems that Maths is not your line.'
A row of textbooks one by one
Achieves the purest neutral dun.
'Why not while you've time to spare
Give it up and try elsewhere?'
And though I'll never quite observe
The beauties of the Gaussian Curve,
Nor find my way through institutions
With warm Bi-modal Distributions,
Nor ever quite hear in my ears
The perfect Music of the Spheres,
I am, for the moment, far from despair—
Walking on lino . . . and on air.

In Dante's Hell

In Dante's Hell
the talk goes on
of southern slopes
and vignerons.

They tread a separate
circle there,
the wine-snobs parched
in their despair.

The floors are wide
with stately tables
bearing wine
of peerless label;

the walls go up
in serried racks
of noble imports
free from tax;

the air is rich
with stilton, brie
and camembert
from Normandy.

Like inmates of
some dismal camp
they circle lit
by discreet lamps

and talk of all
the classic years
and cannot quite
hold back their tears

when reminiscing
on all those
varietal wines
with 'lovely nose',

the late-picked rieslings
'autumn-scented',
the heady moselles
cold-fermented,

the 'bigness' of
a certain red
and what might follow
it in bed.

Their terms for him
who set them here
are those they once
reserved for beer.

And as their looks
grow more accusing
they do not find
the wines 'amusing'

for Satan lets them
talk and think,
do everything
in fact but drink

the vintages
from his high store.
'To drink', he says,
'would surely bore.

A lifetime spent
in love with talk—
what need is there
to draw the cork?'

And so they ferment
two by two
and pay Beelze-
bub his due.

Their talk is muted,
sad and dry
and not a little
anguished by

the upper circle
howls of pain
from puritans on
French champagne.

Andrew Taylor

How to Spend New Year's Eve Alone

Andrew ambles along awkward and all anyhow
bemused by butterflies but bothered by Beate
conjuring contemporary cadences and catchcries
designed to dull or diminish distance and despair.
Eventually everything emerges
frighteningly forceful for effeminate ephebes
guided generally by good grace and generosity.
Highlighting the hiatus
in their intense but international involvement,
genuinely jaundicing Jeremiads and jejune
calamitous catastrophes collapse on him, karate-like,
like limbs of elms, like lightning,
muttering malignant maledictions and murder!
No!
No! No! No!
Only oblivion!
Perhaps
quite quirky but quintessential qualities,
recognised in recondite research but rarely revealed
and seldom scrutinised,
told him of twosomes and of tomorrows together
unspoiled and undivided, and unusually euphoric?
Valiant volition, but vain.
Wagnerian wizardry, world-wobbling worries, wishful wondering,
   the works,
expire around him exhausted, exasperated, in extremis,
yielding, yes yeastily yielding their yondermost yen,
the enzyme zero, the zed of Zen.

Whistling in the Dark

Tonight
all the nectarines will ripen
and not one fall from the tree

Berlioz will sing at my supper
and Mozart with his magic flute
will play for me

at midnight the postman will call with a letter from you
he'll have run all the way from Melbourne
and Freud too will be wrong
about the death of one's father

when I go to bed
there'll be free tickets for the Vienna State Opera
while the price of books will come down
mine will sell fantastically well
my publisher will get a knighthood
tonight

meanwhile

Fred will love me and I'll love her and
Esther will love me and I'll love her and
Roberta will love me and I'll love her and
we'll all love each other and all be terribly happy

and the hens will lay again
two big eggs which I'll hoard until breakfast
and in the morning they'll have grown legs and arms
and one will have taken up knitting
and the other's studying typing and shorthand
because they want their children to have a good education
and no sacrifice is too great

and it will be winter
and I can wear my fur hat and 20 foot scarf
and feel like Laocoon
and I'll brush the snow from my eyes
and when I talk my words will freeze like chords in the frost
then fall to the ground and smash into springs
and fireflies and mushrooms and 20 peso pieces

and every taxi will charge me by the meter
and the Italian barman I once threw a bottle of beer at
will confess he was overcharging

I'll learn to swim
(or at least to keep afloat)
and I'll be able to warn the poor buggers
don't touch that wooden horse it's full of Greeks as a fish shop
and they'll believe me and set fire to it
and sail off and found Rome anyway
being basically adventurous and creative
and tell Michelangelo and Catullus
and Virgil and a whole succession of Popes
they owe it all to me

the loo will stop leaking
and the parrots will all come back
and the bantams will sing and be happy and stop being paranoid
they'll make friends with the pheasants
and do little dances when they lay eggs
and lay eggs

tonight in fact
will be like any other

Dido
burning like a full moon on the horizon
and the song of the sail
heading
for where?

Rae Desmond Jones

aviatrix

(for anne and denis)

1

lindbergh flew
through the night
fighting the atlantic

the black sea glistened
rippled & sucked
almost breathing below

with one hand
on the stick & the other
on his stork he kept

his mind on the
folies bergeres

2

vrrroomm—
O black panties vrr
oomm—shit their

arses dance around
the altimeter vrroo
omm—glinting luminous

as a stage vrooom
mm—dropping now
low humps and hangars

vrrrooomm—paris
O shit

altimeter dropping
i am coming vrrooo
mm—into land

3

although many women
were strangely &
strongly attracted to
him yet he always
remained aloof & modest
& some reporters
commented on his
secretive & charming
smile

4

charles kingsford-
smith was famous
because he was named

after an aerodrome
also he once

crawled out onto
the wing of a flying
plane

over the equator
& looked down & said
i don't see

any bananas

5

amy johnson was
amy johnson &
sounds rather like

a distant aunt

the smell of
powder & perfume
the ack-ack

patterns of lace
under glass & old

photographs

6

jets don't go
vrrooomm—

Nigel Roberts

The Kiwi Riposte

Whats new
in Sydney
mate?

Mens groups
Mens C/R groups,
Mens Consciousness
Raising Groups.

Amazing,
we've had them
here for years
ah well
another case
of what NZ does
Sydney
and then soon
California
will follow
but here
brother
comrade
digger/sport

we call them
Rugby Clubs.

After/the Moratorium Reading

the marie antoinette / slice
of cake / was
awarded to—
who ever said
after this reading / let's
get it on / at Michael's place / I heard
that guy
from Canberra's got
some farout
vietnamese
shit.

Peter Corris

A History of Australia

(C. M. H. Clark)

Five vols down and one to go
Clark puts on a mighty show.
See—men of God and men of Mammon
Make it through the years of famine:
Grow the wheat, the spuds and vino,
Ride upon the great Merino.

Enlightened gentry faking rules
In Parliament for knaves and fools.
Painters, poets make brave bids,
The motto remains: 'Make quick quids'.
Left and right deny all failure
But agree on White Australia.

Eventually, we're Federated
(Queenslanders the least placated).
Trouble is, things are Boering
So we do a bit of warring.
Deakin, Lawson find life murky,
Many die on beach in Turkey.

Ian Reid

What Goes Up Has Further to Come Down

In Australia there are 451 kinds of gum tree.
Reference books list 450; but that ignores
the mutant in Alfred's garden.
It has a sideways habit,
keeps a low profile, seems nostalgic for the underground,
was probably born beneath an earth-sign,
is the one and only *eucalyptus horizontalis*.

He has tried everything to coax it up:
being tied to a stake,
warm showers,
hypnotherapy, poems, the lot.

'Stop fretting, Alf,' says Grace,
'the world's not short of perpendiculars
and who needs them?—
All so straight, so downright upright!'

So under the lateral shade
Alfred and Grace lie gently down together.

John Tranter

Telephone

You know it's dumb hippie magic, but you try
the Zen Bingo Method of Prediction
developed by a gambling vet for the Womens Weekly.
Your girl-friend goes catatonic
and leaves home, so you burst into tears
like a pop star. 'You will grow old, then die.'
So what? The morning after you have trouble
focussing, it's a vertigo attack but you're soon
rehearsing a complex language of invective
that you must have learned in your sleep,
a dialect so eloquent it fills your day
with its brilliant and torrential speech
then you put your clothes on back to front—
it's in 'My Book of Silly Things To Do'—
and the Pop Rocks go off in your mouth,
that's the Chinese Breakfast coming into fashion
and you're feeling great; at least
better than yesterday—remember that?
Those terrible things you said, and the way
they looked at your fit of temper then
looked away—remember? Good, now
things fall into their special place:
that blonde falling down the stairs
of the restaurant, the famous book
falling open at the page where your name
appears as the main suspect, and the handset
dangling from its cord saying 'dial-tone',
'dial-tone' until you could scream.
Somewhere very far away somebody's laughing
and laughing. You are older than you were before.

Channel Nothing

for the Subtitlers at SBS-TV

The TV's full of Norwegian banter
like a soundtrack going backwards and just
off-screen a drunk falls into the cake
    but nobody moves:

that is, they move from the Nordic
state of doubt to the Arabic then
back again via Disneyland and if you
    blink you miss it

like the subtitle you thought you saw:
'I couldn't help giving birth to a Negro!'
or the landscape painting titled
    'Bruce Buys a Truck'—

you're there at the edge of the frame
wearing a smile and waving. Things look
odd from the top of a truck—lurid, somehow,
    blurred by speed

and badly out of focus like the alcoholic
sliding down through the print
that brands his forehead with the
    odd marriage customs

of the Norsemen and their tawny guests.
Is that a lion? Or a Bantu 'being' a lion?
Come out, Simba! Bruce the White Hunter sleeps
    under the table tonight.

Mark O'Connor

The Gorilla and I

(a guitar poem)

Well I was walking down a pathway
  that they let the tourists use,
through the last big bit of jungle
  the bulldozers haven't moved.

So I'd taken off my gumboots
  and I'd thrown away my clothes,
and I'd stepped up on a tree-stump
  when I heard a voice quite close.

You seem a hairy fellow
  and you've stepped right off the path,
why don't you come and join us?
  We're the last sane ones on earth.

I sed, 'Mr Gorilla
  it's a chance I've always dreamed,
just to melt into the jungle
  where no man has ever been.

'But where can I find shelter?
  And what food can I eat?
And what bed will you show me
  when I need to rest my feet?'

'My land is all one shelter,
  it's shielded from the sun;
and you'll find sweet grubs and beetles
  in old tree stumps by the ton.

'And when your skin gets tougher
  you'll find every tree's a bed,
where you and a chosen female
  can help our nation spred.'

'Your females wouldn't suit me
  since I'm fixed on hairless blondes;
and I happen to know they're replacing
  your trees with some sewerage ponds.'

He sed, 'Well I suppose you know
 how your own damnation feels;
it's a shame you couldn't help us
 but I guess that sets the seal.'

Just then some Yankee tourists
 came chattering down the track,
and he zipped off in the forest
 just as sharp as a rifle crack.

But I met him three months later
 in some sportsman's trophy hall;
with his wife turned out beside him
 and tacked up on the wall.

And I've often wished I'd told him
 what he really ought to do:
he'd have had much better prospects
 if he'd signed up with a zoo.

Wheaties: an Alphabetical Parody

Alive, aloof, aloft, brisk, bright, bundled, brindled,
flakes crisp, crunch, crush, crash, dash and dangle-dive; fire
flight, float, flit, flip, are flash-foundered, fondled
(O pity and indignation!) to the gyre
plate-prison of greedy, grasping, milky curd:
gray, grey, gruesome, gooey, how it gathers to a gush
of horrible hot hebetude! and stirred
when slishy, sloshy sugar turns to slush!

Flakes steeped and pashed quite in love-lace slush:
generations have stirred, have stirred, have stirred
its ripe bran-flesh sent seething to a holy hush.
but O thou my (Hup!) flesh-fretted god-Guy Word
back-buy us from man's soggy saccharine food,
let lip know heart's ambrosia having been back-wooed.

Riding a Hired Lambretta in the Fifth Lane of the Autostrada to Visit the Underworld . . .

Descent into Hell! It was like a Fellini film.
All day seeking the Sibyl's cave we ricocheted
through a stream of cars, like crazed projectiles
aimed for the drive-in beach resorts of that shore
where Aeneas landed. Fat-bottomed boppers
in wispy bikinis pointed hopefully on: 'Just past
the nude-beach carpark. Like a ticket to swim?'

Old poets believed
that the entrance to Hell was known and easy—
the She-Prophet's Cave near Cumae. But to return
to the winds and the light of the surface
was hard and uncertain.

You could smell the Naples water. In the land
of volcanic and mechanic sulphur whose surface
bubbles and smokes, sinks and resounds
hollowly when struck, we passed the Avernus
Riding School and Bar, and the Stygian Tomato
Co-op. Buy Lethe! The God's last word:
'leave nothing in your car'.

John A. Scott

When Things Go Wrong (They All Go Wrong)

(To music by Robert Moore)

When things go wrong, they all go wrong,
The hand of friendship is King Kong's,
Pains in the head, son's wet the bed,
   The parrot's dead.

It never rains, it only pours,
Not cats-and-dogs, but dinosaurs!
There's Noah's Ark across the park.
   It's getting dark.

When I think of all the misery just waiting for me,
If I ever had to go outside, I'd probably suicide.

And now my wife is in the car,
She's packed her bags and said ta-ta!
She's going abroad, I'm being ignored.
   She says she's bored.

NIP

(for Alan Wearne)

Another night of television
Spoilt by violence. For ten minutes
The weekly gardener's guide
Spelled death to the state of things,
As a weather-beaten anarchist
In boots leered at a thousand
Living-rooms, and announced
With uncommon calm: 'tonight we're
Going to do a bit of pruning . . .'

The tree, no longer the steady
Diagram of life, language & family,
Stood before us like a vast
Political structure: and sure enough
Just as we sat back, assured
In its strength, there began
A series of violent coups:
'Here's a leader that's going
In a wrong direction . . .'

The words no sooner left his mouth,
Than with a crisp and decisive
Nip, months of peaceful
Growth and manoeuvring came
To a sudden end. We sat
Bolt upright in our recliners.
'Now here's a weak leader. We'll
Remove him . . .' and the blades
Set about their deadly task.

The next morning, I spent
Some time in the garden: admiring
The ramshackle status-quo
Wondering if all revolutions
Were as easy as that! Great
Or lesser tyrants, quaking
At the historical secateurs.
'Without change there is no progress'
I declared. 'Power tends to corrupt'
The pear-tree watched me
Unsteadily from near the gate.

Man in Petersham

He's dropped his heart!
His heart has fallen to the footpath.
But no-one seems surprised and least of all
the office girl whose stockings violin
across this empty road. He's dropped his heart!
It surely must be this and not his cigarettes.
The way he stares so long and makes no effort
to redeem it. And his suit is an immaculate grey,
and his shoes a duco white. And his feet are
frozen in the tiny refrigerators of his shoes.
With all the colours running out, he stares
upon his fallen heart. His mild-blue heart
shattered in its twenty filtered pieces.

John Clarke

'Fifteen Bobsworth Longfellow'

Fifteen Bobsworth Longfellow was an Adelaide academic who wrote instructions for kit-set model products, mainly balsa wood aircraft and submarines which ran on baking powder. The manual included here was for the assembling of a 25 foot Aircraft Carrier marketed by Myer stores between 1954 and 1960.

Myer's Whopper

Take the pieces from the package,
Lay them out as per the graph,
Gathering the bits you'll need,
Removing what you shouldn't have.
With the implement provided
Ease the bearings to the left,
Push the little angled mullion
Up into the socket 'F'.
This will free the moulded bracket
Holding back the nylon strand,
Draw the slippery hoop and coupling
Through the right-hand rubber-band.
Put the topside brown side outside,
Push the inside upside down,
Underneath the left-hand wingnut,
Press the folding backward crown.
Overlapping lifting side-flaps
Lower in to fit the screws,
Pack up tools, retire to distance,
Don protective hat, light fuse.

Ted Lear

Ted Lear popularised limericks in his 'A Book of Rubbish', although tragically he failed to recognise that the way to make them work was to have a filthy last line. As well as writing limericks, Ted Lear has left us with some of the most enchanting nonsense verse in the language.

The Pibbledy-Pobbledy Man

When the Yonghy Bonghy's singly fat
On the coast of the Fimbly Far,
And the beauteous Lady Jingly's hat
Looks up at the evening star.
He weeps alone on the shingly shore,
He pumpkinly goes for a walk,
Drinks his marsala through calico straws,
He haveth a runcible dork.

Rapidly numerous,
Vapidly humorous,
He mourns with a sweet guitar,
The wonderful pussy is loved by the owl
Who feels a complete galah.
When the Yonghy Bonghy has lost his way,
The birds make a nest in his beard,
He sits in the afternoon tea tree,
And regrets it is just as he feared.

Jamie Grant

A First View of Cricket

What use is this ritual, held
   on a circular meadow
with men arranged in clusters, some
   almost out of earshot? They
all wear cream flannel trousers:
   perhaps they're hospital
orderlies, or homosexuals.

A group of them lie on the grass,
   and one is scribbling notes
on sheets of green paper. Another
   climbs to his feet, then stoops
down beneath the railings—his brow
   inscribed with innocent hope
reminds me of our priests, inviting

God's assistance with the harvest.
   He cradles a wooden object
in his arms, that's a sculpted
   delicate wedge shape which seems
to me quite useless as a tool.
   Blue laminex sky, where clouds
unreel like bolts of flannel.

Air so still the noises made
   by birds echo in a vacant
corridor. Now, that man
   attempts to dig a furrow
with his unsuitable implement—
   someone rushes at him
and swings both arms like the arms

of a metronome. And he leaves the trench
   unfinished: when he reaches
the place he set out from, his
   expression is utterly changed,
the face of a man returned
   from a long and serious journey,
returned to a punitive silence.

Richard Tipping

Capt Cook Considers His Fete

When he sailed in, (his head filled with his
mother's warnings, tensing his sealegs, his
worrybeads worrying, screwing and unscrewing his
shining telescope, watching the Natives watching his
ship), the full significance of his present reactions
escaped him completely

Mangoes

mangoes are not cigarettes
mangoes are fleshy skinful passionate fruits
mangoes are hungry to be sucked
mangoes are glad to be stuck in the teeth
mangoes like slush & kissing

mangoes are not cigarettes
mangoes are idiosyncratic seasonal seducers
mangoes are worse than adams apple
mangoes are what parents & parliamentarians warn against
mangoes like making rude noises

mangoes are not filter tipped
mangoes are greedy delicious tongueteasers
mangoes are violently soft
mangoes are fibrous intestinal lovebites
mangoes like beginning once again

mangoes are not cigarettes
mangoes are tangible sensual intelligence
mangoes are debauched antisocialites
mangoes are a positive good in the world
mangoes like poetry

When You're Feeling Kind of Bonkers

When you're feeling kind of bonkers—
Got a screw loose, round the bend;
When you're crazed, berserk, gone potty,
Don't know really from pretend;

You'll be flipped out, stung, bananas,
Off your rocker, flicking nuts,
'Cause the booby-hatch and loony bin
Can't dot the 'i' on all your buts;

When you've gone completely ga-ga,
Chewed the razor, up the pole,
Non compos mentis, out the window,
Now the moon is full and cold;

You'll be happy, second childhood,
Mad-stark raving, whacky, bats,
One hand clapping, wave to dada—
And finally, totally, crack.

Peter Goldsworthy

Jokes

Don't tell me jokes,
I know about jokes.
They think they are funny.
They think they can get away with things.

I don't know everything about them,
just enough. I know this:
that they refuse to be remembered,
slipping the mind's fingers,
a shoal of laughter, vanishing.

And this: that they hide still inside,
deeply. Delinquent poems,
absconders from custody.

Of course they think it a great lark,
sneaking back again and again:
the grenade of laughter,
then silence.
I prefer to find it tiresome.
And a little sad.
All that repetition!

Don't pigeon-hole me:
I appreciate a good joke.
I said appreciate, not laugh at.
For I will no longer laugh.
I will not answer their ridiculous summons,
I refuse to accept their subpoena.
Never again will I eagerly rip open
the scented envelope
filled with strange plastic.

There are only four jokes anyway:
the custard pie, and the breaking of taboo,
the game of words, and the thing
we are each most afraid of.

Allan Jurd

Part 1

becoming obnoxious on a television evening

TVs are so very romantic,
a war movie was on
i dropped the half bottle of beer
on the floor as i was putting
it back in the frig
'careful' my wife screamed
'Don't worry' i said
'It's not coca-cola'
just then a soft drink ad fizzed on to the screen
my beer was valid

Part 2

they all say square eyes, but it's a square area

i had the headphones on,
this silence really sorted out
the actors, like silent movies.
the crook had a smug look
'He's a smart arse' i said
'SHUT UP' everyone said
which gave the crook
time to escape.

Chris Mansell

Definition Poem: Pissed as a Parrot

For those of you who are etymologically inclined
I would like to take this opportunity
to explain to you the derivation of the expression
pissed as a parrot.

Sidney Baker in *The Australian Language* indexes
  Paroo dog
  Parrot
  Parson's pox
There is no entry under *pissed.*
He also gives
  Proverbial, come the
  Piss, panther's
and Pseudoxy.

Parrot on page 55 is a sheep
which has lost some of its wool.
If the sheep's flyblown it's a rosella.

Wilkes in his *Australian Dictionary of Colloquialisms*
lists only to piss in someone's pocket
(refer Kylie Tennant, Bray, Hardy & Herbert)
Pissant around (Dymphna Cusack)
and Pissant, game as a.
There is no mention of any parrot in any condition at all.

In *Collins English Dictionary* (Australian Edition)
you will find definitions for
  piss
  piss about
  Pissaro
  piss artist
and piss off.

Parrots appear in their psittaciformes capacity
which I found meant having a short hooked bill,
compact body, bright plumage, and an ability
to mimic.
It was not entirely clear whether this referred to birds.

Parrot fashion had nothing to do with anything.

Roget's *Thesaurus*
Nuttal's *Dictionary of Synonyms and Antonyms*
Stillman's *Poets Manual and Rhyming Dictionary*
Webster's *Treasury of Synonyms, Antonyms and Homonyms*
and the *Shorter Oxford English Dictionary*
were no help at all.

I thought *Usage and Abusage*
being by Partridge
could be illuminating, but it appears
that neither piss nor parrots are abused.

I refused to consult Strunk's *Elements of Style*
on the grounds that the backcover blurb
has quotes from the *Greensboro Daily News*
and *The Telephone Engineers and Management Journal.*

But I went to afternoon tea
in the School of Chemistry at the University of Sydney
at 4 p.m. on Thursday 6 November
and there, Dr A. R. Lacey, physical chemist, MSc, PhD,
informed me, in his capacity as a true blue,
down to earth, dinky-di, grass roots Aussie that
when working on his horse stud in the Wingecarribee Shire
he had observed that Gang Gang cockatoos
fall with paralytic suddenness
from the branches of Hawthorn bushes
after ingesting the berries.

Incredibly, *The Reader's Digest Complete Book of Australian Birds*
makes no mention of this.

Kevin Hart

'Till Sotell Deth Knoked At My Gate'

Don't let him think you're home: lock all the doors,
cut off the telephone, and plug both ears;
divorce your wife—she might make a mistake;
let all your mail pile up outside; put out
some bottles of rancid milk beside the gate.

You must let paint peel from the walls, and grass
run riot till it chokes the garden beds.
Ensure the lights won't work; a rat or two
about the place will make the thing seem real;
a phoney grave in your front lawn might help

(but make sure it looks old, he's wise to this).
Forget your friends, tell them you've gone away,
and pray that they won't think to do the same:
this plan will only work for one or two.
Be scrupulous, the whole thing must look right,

no, perfect, if it is to work at all.
Think of him constantly—and scratch his name
upon your glasses so you won't forget;
eat from a coffin lid, and sleep inside.
Be vigilant, he comes by all the time.

I almost forgot—check that he doesn't know
your face already—think if anyone
has died inside your place: a father, child,
or dog perhaps—could he have seen you then?
If so, it's necessary you move at once.

You've got it all? Good, good. Now off you go.
Remember, if it fails you don't know me,
you don't know where I live—perhaps it's best
to say I went to live in Mexico.
We shall not meet again. Good luck my friend.

John Denman

The Dying Treasurer

(Tune: The Dying Stockman)

A Federal Treasurer lay dying,
His budget supporting his head.
The Cabinet stood plausibly lying
As he raised on his elbow and said:

Chorus

Wrap me up in my jiggery-pokery,
Wrap me round in my legerdemain.
Bury me deep in the rhetoric
Right next to the monetary drain.

There's booze in the cut-glass decanter,
Place the tumblers all in a row
And toast more and more unemployment—
May the total continue to grow.

Cut down the Consumer Price Index
Put wages and salaries on ice.
Lock up one or two union leaders
To help me attain paradise.

Oh, had I the flight of a bronze-wing
Instead of a blind silver-tail,
I'd fly in the face of all reason
And I'd write my last budget in Braille.

ACKNOWLEDGEMENTS

We wish to thank the following copyright-holders for permission to use the following material:
Anonymous: 'Sausage Wrap Serenade' and 'The Song of the RSL' from *The Balls of Bob Menzies—Australian Political Songs 1900–1980*, by Warren Fahey, Angus & Robertson. Dorothy Auchterlonie: 'Insomniacs, Please Note', by permission of Andrew Green and Harriet Jungheim, coexecutors of the estate of the late Dorothy Green. John Blight: 'The Glove' from *Pageantry for a Lost Empire*, Nelson, 1977. John Bray: 'The Birds on North Terrace' and 'St George and the Dragon Discussion Group' from *Poems 1961–1971*, Jacaranda Press, 1972; 'Non Event' from *Poems 1977–1979*, Australian National University Press; 'Dilemma' and 'Entomology and Below'. R. F. Brissenden: 'Zoology AO1' from *The Whale in Darkness*, Australian National University Press, 1980; 'The Canberra Blues', 'The Back-Blocks Academic' and 'With a Glass of Spaetlaese' from *Gough & Johnny Were Lovers*, Penguin, 1984. Vincent Buckley: 'Teaching German Literature' from *Last Poems*, McPhee Gribble, 1991. David Campbell: 'Small-Town Gladys', 'Jack Spring', 'The Australian Dream', 'The Tourist Trade', 'Canberra Incident' and 'Mothers and Daughters' from *David Campbell: Collected Poems*, Angus & Robertson, 1989. John Clarke: 'Myer's Whopper' and 'The Pibbledy-Pobbledy Man' from *The Complete Book of Australian Verse by John Clarke*, Allen & Unwin Haynes, 1989. Marcus Clarke: 'The Wail of the Waiter'. Peter Corris: 'A History of Australia' from *The Flight of the Emu*, Angus & Robertson, 1990. Alexander Craig: 'The Silver Screw'. Dennis Davison: 'To Her Coy Lover' and 'Mrs Homer T. Mickiewicz' from *Poetry Monash*. Bruce Dawe: 'Weather Forecast', 'Genesis' and 'Under a Cloud' from *Just a Dugong at Twilight*, Cheshire, Melbourne, 1968; 'Lights! Lights!' from *Beyond the Subdivisions*, Cheshire, Melbourne, 1969; 'On the Conferring of an Honorary Doctorate of Law on a Politician' from *An Eye for a Tooth*, Cheshire, Melbourne, 1968. John Denman: 'The Dying Treasurer' from *The Balls of Bob Menzies—Australian Political Songs 1900–1980*, by Warren Fahey, Angus & Robertson. Rosemary Dobson: 'Piltdown Man', 'Oracles for a Childhood Journey', 'Carried Away' and 'Captain Svenson' from *Collected Poems*, Angus & Robertson, 1973; 'Closed Museums'. Geoffrey Dutton: 'Our Crypto-Wowsers' and 'Our Leisured Ladies'. Robert D. FitzGerald: 'Favour' from *40 Years Poems*. Leon Gellert: 'The Kangaroo', 'The Mutton-Bird' and 'The Platypus' from *Beastly Australians*, Hodder

& Stoughton, 1964. Barbara Giles: 'Pretty Ditty' from *Poetry Monash* No. 10, 1981 (Light Verse Issue); 'O Oedipus! O Mores!' first published in *Nation Review*; 'To All Hereditary Princes' from *Eve Rejects Apple*, Angus & Robertson. Peter Goldsworthy: 'Jokes' from *Selected Poems*, Angus & Robertson, 1991. W. T. Goodge: 'A Bad Break!' and 'The M'Camley Mixture'. John Goss: 'Williamanmary, the Cat', first published in *Smith's Weekly*, 1937; 'Fiat Justitia'. Jamie Grant: 'A First View of Cricket'. Philip Grundy: 'Hymn to Canberra, Queen of the Plains and Hills' and 'A Democratic Benefaction'. Lesbia Harford: 'Skirt Machinist'. Keith Harrison: 'Picasso's Bull'. Kevin Hart: 'Till Sotell Deth Knoked at My Gate' from *Your Shadow*, Angus & Robertson. Gwen Harwood: 'Out of Hell'; 'Schrödinger's Cat Preaches to the Mice' and 'Blackbird' from *Bone Scan*, Angus & Robertson, 1988; 'The Flight of the Bumble Bee' and 'A Small Victory' from *Selected Poems*, Angus & Robertson, 1985. A. D. Hope: 'To Julia Walking Away', 'The House of God', 'The Brides' and 'Clover Honey' from *Collected Poems*, Angus & Robertson. Clive James: 'The Book of My Enemy Has Been Remaindered' and 'Will Those Responsible Please Come Forward?' from *Other Passports*, Jonathan Cape, 1986.Rae Desmond Jones: 'aviatrix' from *The Mad Vibe*, Saturday Centre Press, 1975. Allan Jurd: 'Part 1' and Part 2'. Nancy Kessing: 'Procedures' and 'Reflections of a Guest Speaker'. Henry Lawson: 'Rise Ye! Rise Ye!. Norman Lindsay: 'The Penguin Bold'. John Manifold: 'The Sirens', 'Chillianwallah Station', 'Outer Suburbs' and 'Musicians' from *Collected Verse*, University of Queensland Press, 1978. Chris Mansell: 'Definition Poem: Pissed as a Parrot'. Philip Martin: 'Bequest' from *A Bone Flute*, Australian National University Press, 1974; 'Thanks for the Stockings'. James McAuley: 'Jindyworobaksheesh', 'The True Discovery of Australia', 'The Convict and the Lady' and 'Tabletalk' from *Collected Poems 1936–1970*, Angus & Robertson, 1971. Ronald McCuaig: 'Pretty Kid' and 'The Letter' from *Quod Ronald McCuaig*, Angus & Robertson, 1946. Hector Monro: 'You'll Love Their Fubsy, Tangy Charm', 'Faith Before Birth'; 'Fundamentalist', 'Modernist' and 'The Mystic East' from *A Short Guide to Religion*; 'Aristotle', 'Karl Marx' and 'Bertrand Russell' from *The Sonneteer's History of Philosophy*, all reprinted by permission of Hector Monro and with acknowledgements to the Ancora Press, *Poetry Monash*, *The Monash Reporter* and *The Australian Rationalist Quarterly*. E. G. Murphy: 'Thank you, Mr Rason, for the Apples'. John Shaw Neilson: 'The Case of Adam' from *Selected Poems*, Angus & Robertson. Mark O'Connor: 'The Gorilla and I', 'Wheaties: An Alphabetical Parody' and 'Riding a Hired Lambretta in the Fifth Lane of the Autostrada to Visit the Underworld' courtesy of the poet c/o Curtis Brown (Aust) Pty Ltd, Sydney.

Geoff Page: 'A Toper Speaks' and 'In Dante's Hell' from *Clairvoyant in Autumn*, Angus & Robertson, 1983; 'Giving It Up' reprinted by permission of Geoff Page. A. B. Paterson: 'The Lost Leichhardt' from *Selected Poems*, Angus & Robertson. Grace Perry: 'Canberra City Sunday' from South Head Press. Peter Porter: 'A Consumer's Report' from *Collected Poems*, Oxford University Press, 1983; 'A Bag of Pressmints' from *The Automatic Oracle*, Oxford University Press, 1987. Ian Reid: 'What Goes Up Has Further to Come Down' reprinted by permission of Ian Reid. Nigel Roberts: 'The Kiwi Riposte' from Hale & Iremonger; 'After/the Moratorium Reading', reprinted by permission of Nigel Roberts. Isobel Robin: 'The Invitreous Advent of Septimus'; 'Frogs' Eggs'. John A. Scott: 'When Things Go Wrong (They All Go Wrong)' and 'NIP' from *The Flooded City*, Makar Press, 1981, reprinted by permission of John A. Scott; 'Man in Petersham' from *Singles*, 1989. Kenneth Slessor: 'Skies and Skis' and 'Eating by Yourself' from *Backless Betty from Bondi*, Angus & Robertson, 1983. Andrew Taylor: 'How to Spend New Year's Eve Alone' and 'Whistling in the Dark' from *Selected Poems*, University of Queensland Press, 1982. Richard Tipping: 'Captain Cook Considers His Fete' from *Soft Riot*, Paperback Poets 10, University of Queensland Press, 1972; 'Mangoes' from *Domestic Hardcore*, Paperback Poets second series 9, University of Queensland Press, 1975; 'When You're Feeling Kind of Bonkers', all reprinted by permission of Richard Tipping. John Tranter: 'Telephone' from *Selected Poems*, Hale & Iremonger, 1990; *Dazed in the Ladies Lounge*, Island Press, Sydney, 1979; 'Channel Nothing'. Dimitris Tsaloumas: 'CHOGM—Melbourne 1981' from *The Book of Epigrams*, University of Queensland Press, 1985. Chris Wallace-Crabbe: 'Exit the Players' first published in *Southerly*, Oxford University Press, courtesy of Chris Wallace-Crabbe; 'Citizen' and 'The Collective Invention' from *Selected Poems*, Angus & Robertson and Chris Wallace-Crabbe; 'Whisky' first published in *Poetry Review*, courtesy of Chris Wallace-Crabbe and the Editor of *Poetry Review*. Judith Wright: 'The True Religion' first published in *The Australian*/*The Sydney Morning Herald*, reprinted by permission of Judith Wright.

Details for the acknowledgements are as supplied by the editor and copyright-holders. Every effort has been made to trace the original source of all material contained in this book. Where the attempt has been unsuccessful the editor and publisher would be pleased to hear from the author/publisher concerned, to rectify any omission.

Index of First Lines

Index of Authors and Titles